NEW DIRECTIONS FOR HIGHER EDUCATION

Martin Kramer
EDITOR-IN-CHIEF

Changing Student Attendance Patterns
Challenges for Policy and Practice

Jacqueline E. King
American Council on Education

Eugene L. Anderson
American Council on Education

Melanie E. Corrigan
American Council on Education

EDITORS

Number 121, Spring 2003

JOSSEY-BASS
San Francisco

CHANGING STUDENT ATTENDANCE PATTERNS: CHALLENGES FOR POLICY AND PRACTICE
Jacqueline E. King, Eugene L. Anderson, Melanie E. Corrigan (eds.)
New Directions for Higher Education, no. 121
Martin Kramer, Editor-in-Chief

Microfilm copies of issues and articles are available in 16mm and 35mm, as well as microfiche in 105mm, through University Microfilms Inc., 300 North Zeeb Road, Ann Arbor, Michigan 48106-1346.

ISSN 0271-0560   electronic ISSN 1536-0741

NEW DIRECTIONS FOR HIGHER EDUCATION is part of The Jossey-Bass Higher and Adult Education Series and is published quarterly by Wiley Subscription Services, Inc., a Wiley company, at Jossey-Bass, 989 Market Street, San Francisco, California 94103-1741. Periodicals postage paid at San Francisco, California, and at additional mailing offices. Postmaster: Send address changes to New Directions for Higher Education, Jossey-Bass, 989 Market Street, San Francisco, California 94103-1741.

New Directions for Higher Education is indexed in Current Index to Journals in Education (ERIC); Higher Education Abstracts.

SUBSCRIPTIONS cost $70 for individuals and $145 for institutions, agencies, and libraries. See ordering information page at end of book.

EDITORIAL CORRESPONDENCE should be sent to the Editor-in-Chief, Martin Kramer, 2807 Shasta Road, Berkeley, California 94708-2011.

Cover photograph and random dot by Richard Blair/Color & Light © 1990.

www.josseybass.com

CONTENTS

EDITORS' NOTES   1
Jacqueline E. King, Eugene L. Anderson, Melanie E. Corrigan

1. Changing U.S. Demographics and American Higher   3
Education
Eugene L. Anderson
As America changes, so does demand for higher education. Ethnic
diversity and the "Baby Boom Echo" generation's entry into college are
among the trends that will change student profiles.

2. Swirling and Double-Dipping: New Patterns of Student   13
Attendance and Their Implications for Higher Education
Alexander C. McCormick
Attendance at multiple institutions is increasingly common and
involves a number of patterns beside transfers between institutions.

3. Beyond Access: Persistence Challenges and the Diversity of   25
Low-Income Students
Melanie E. Corrigan
Low-income students enter higher education with family obligations
and goals that often vary from those of their younger and traditional
counterparts and that make persistence much more challenging.

4. New Modes of Productivity for Student Learning   35
Barbara E. Walvoord
To make productivity strategies work, an institution needs to put in
place a program of five components: learning goals, measures of student performance, knowledge of how to achieve learning with the particular student population, knowledge of options for increasing
productivity, and institution-wide support.

5. Public Policy Implications of Changing Student Attendance   51
Patterns
David A. Longanecker, Cheryl D. Blanco
Public policy can respond to changing student attendance patterns in
four ways: funding programs, contracting with private entities to provide services, creating incentives for private action, and mandating
action through law or regulations.

6. Nontraditional Attendance and Persistence: The Cost of   69
Students' Choices
Jacqueline E. King
Working more than part-time and attending college part-time negatively affect persistence—especially for low-income students. These student choices also impede the ability of institutions to shorten
time-to-degree, improve graduation rates, and accommodate larger
numbers of students.

7. Rethinking Policy, Process, and Planning to Redefine Quality   85
and Enhance Student Success
Joanne Passaro, Lucie Lapovsky, Louise H. Feroe, James R. Metzger
Combining broad access with academic excellence requires a carefully
articulated set of academic and support strategies and practices that can
pinpoint student needs and target appropriate resources.

8. Best Practices in Providing Nontraditional Students with   99
Both Academic and Financial Support
Natala K. Hart
Reducing the time that students must spend in the financial aid office
and integrating financial and academic advising are especially helpful
to nontraditional students.

INDEX   107

EDITORS' NOTES

The American college population is becoming more diverse in race-ethnicity, socioeconomic status, and age. In addition, students are taking part in higher education in increasingly diverse ways. They are working, attending part-time, and moving between institutions in increasing numbers. The data are no less than astonishing. Eighty percent of undergraduates work while enrolled, half attend part-time, and 60 percent of bachelor's degree recipients have attended more than one institution during their undergraduate careers. Further, 75 percent of undergraduates possess at least one nontraditional characteristic (such as attending part-time or being a parent) that is associated with a decreased likelihood of persistence to a degree.

These data raise myriad questions for higher education. What are the effects of this new reality on the quality of the student experience? Which students are more likely to attend college in nontraditional ways? How should policymakers and institutions respond to an increasingly nontraditional student population? How do we maintain the soundness and coherence of the academic experience when students move frequently from institution to institution? How can institutions and policymakers best help nontraditional students who have jobs and families to succeed in their academic endeavors?

This volume addresses these questions by examining data on the student experience and calling on experts to offer their perspectives on how policymakers and institutions can accommodate student choices, maintain academic integrity, and promote student success.

The volume begins with three chapters that describe the changing landscape. Eugene Anderson uses data from the 2000 census to outline the demographic shifts that will bring more students of color and older students to college campuses in the years ahead. Alex McCormick describes the phenomenon of multiple-institution attendance, outlining the primary patterns of student behavior and discussing the implications of these patterns for higher education. McCormick raises the very important issue of maintaining a proper balance between the integrity and coherence of academic programs and growing demand among consumers and policymakers for easing transfer and other forms of student mobility. Finally, Melanie Corrigan looks at the special challenges faced by low-income students, concentrating on those characteristics and behaviors that make it particularly difficult for low-income nontraditional students to persist and succeed in higher education.

The next three chapters examine various aspects of the challenge posed by nontraditional students and their changing attendance patterns. Barbara Walvoord describes new ways to structure course work that improve faculty and learner productivity *and* better serve the learning styles and needs of

NEW DIRECTIONS FOR HIGHER EDUCATION, no. 121, Spring 2003 © Wiley Periodicals, Inc.

nontraditional students. David Longanecker and Cheryl Blanco examine the challenges that changing student characteristics and attendance patterns pose for policymakers. They describe how federal and state policies can influence attendance patterns and predict that policymaking will continue to lag behind changes in student characteristics and behavior. Jacqueline King describes how students' financing choices, together with institutional policies and practices in student advising, can impede or facilitate persistence and degree attainment.

The last two chapters present case studies of how two institutions—a midsize private comprehensive college and a large public research university—are addressing the challenges posed by nontraditional students and changing attendance patterns. To promote both access and success for its largely low-income and nontraditional students, Mercy College has undertaken a wholesale reorganization of its support services and redesign of its curricula around core competencies, as Joanne Passaro, Lucie Lapovsky, Louise Feroe, and James Metzger explain in Chapter Seven. To confront the nexus between students' financial decisions and their academic success in a large-scale setting, The Ohio State University has redesigned its financial aid processes, developed minicourses, and brought together financial aid and academic advisers to provide students with one-on-one attention at the most critical junctures, as Natala Hart describes in Chapter Eight.

The challenges and opportunities presented by nontraditional students and their changing attendance patterns are enormous. This volume has only scratched the surface of the issues that higher education institutions and policymakers must confront as they attempt to serve students who combine college with family and work responsibilities and who move frequently between institutions. Nonetheless, the data, informed analysis, and institutional case studies presented here should help higher education officials craft academic and student support policies and programs for individuals whom we still call "nontraditional" but who have actually become typical American college students.

Jacqueline E. King
Eugene L. Anderson
Melanie E. Corrigan
Editors

JACQUELINE E. KING is director of the Center for Policy Analysis at the American Council on Education.

EUGENE L. ANDERSON is a research associate in the Center for Policy Analysis and Office of Minorities in Higher Education at the American Council on Education.

MELANIE E. CORRIGAN is assistant director of the Center for Policy Analysis at the American Council on Education.

1

*Higher education in the United States is more diverse
today because of dramatic shifts in the general population
and increased attendance among adults. These trends will
continue as more adults begin or return to college and as
the Baby Boom Echo generation enters college. Whereas
persons of color will become the new majority in several
states, many states will remain mostly white.*

Changing U.S. Demographics and American Higher Education

Eugene L. Anderson

To set the stage for this volume's discussion of changing student attendance patterns, this chapter describes the demographic shifts in the United States and in higher education. Changing demographics and student attendance patterns pose new challenges for higher education. Three important demographic trends are affecting higher education today and will continue to play a pivotal role in shaping the future of postsecondary education. First, as the children of the Baby Boomers—the generation known as the Baby Boom Echo—enter college over the next fifteen years, the traditional college-age population will expand dramatically. Second, as the United States continues to become more racially diverse—with the increase in the number of people of color far outpacing that of whites in some parts of the country— so will the college population. Finally, the number of adults participating in postsecondary education also continues to increase. Thirty years ago, the overwhelming majority of college students were white and under the age of twenty-five. Today, 28 percent of students are persons of color and a third of undergraduate students are twenty-five years old and older. Recent data suggest that these trends will only grow stronger during the next decade. The increase in older students and students of color creates a variety of challenges for colleges and universities. Several of these challenges will be discussed later in this volume.

The Changing Campus

Since 1970, the number of older adults enrolling in postsecondary education has increased significantly. In 1970, about 2.4 million of America's 8.5 million undergraduate students were twenty-five years old and older. Over the next three decades, the number of older students increased by 144 percent, whereas the number of students under age twenty-five increased by 45 percent. By 1999, 33 percent of postsecondary students were twenty-five and older, an increase of 11 percentage points since 1970. Although this includes students enrolled in graduate degree programs, 71 percent of students age twenty-five and older were undergraduates in 1999. The larger number of these students contributed greatly to the increase in part-time students. From 1970 to 1999 the number of part-time students in higher education rose by 117 percent, compared with 51 percent for full-time students. Of the nearly 6 million postsecondary students age twenty-five and older in 1999, 69 percent were enrolled part-time (U.S Department of Education, 2002). According to the National Center of Educational Statistics (NCES), the number of older college students will continue to increase. By 2012, NCES estimates that 6.6 million college students will be age twenty-five and older (Gerald and Hussar, 2002).

Another trend that is changing the face of higher education is the greater racial-ethnic diversity of students. In 1976, only 16 percent of postsecondary students were minorities. By 1999, 28 percent of all postsecondary students were persons of color. From 1976 to 1999 the number of minorities enrolled in postsecondary institutions increased by 137 percent, compared with an increase of only 13 percent among whites. The large growth in students of color from 1976 to 1999 is due largely to increases in two populations: the number of Asian Americans more than tripled (360 percent growth) and the number of Hispanics more than doubled (243 percent). (It should be noted that the term *Hispanic* refers to all people of that heritage, no matter their race. For the purposes of this chapter, however, the Hispanic population is included in discussions of minority populations.)

From 1976 to 1999, the number of students of color rose by 2.3 million, two times greater than the rise in number of white students. During this period, Hispanics and Asian Americans were responsible for the largest numerical increases (933,000 and 712,000, respectively). The number of African Americans increased by 59 percent, with the numerical increase in these students at more than 600,000. The increase among American Indians was also significant (360 percent); however, because the number of American Indian students enrolled in 1976 was so small the numerical growth from 1976 to 1999 was only 69,000. Higher education will continue to become more racially diverse because the rate of growth among people of color in the United States is significantly higher than for whites. An analysis of the 2000 census (U.S. Census Bureau, 2000) shows that big demographic shifts occurred during the 1990s that will dramatically affect college enrollment in the years ahead.

National Changes

As Table 1.1 shows, in 2000 there were more than 280 million people in the United States, an increase of 13 percent over 1990 (U.S. Census Bureau, 1990, 2000). People of color spurred the growth in the population during the 1990s. The number of whites increased by only 3 percent, whereas the number of people of color increased by 43 percent. Hispanics and Asian Americans, with 58 percent and 52 percent increases in population, respectively, led the growth among people of color. Significant growth also occurred among African Americans (16 percent) and American Indians (15 percent).

The rapid population growth among Hispanics during the 1990s moved them past African Americans as the second largest racial-ethnic group in the country. In 2000, there were more than 35 million Hispanics, compared with nearly 34 million African Americans. The significant growth among Asian Americans increased their numbers from nearly 7 million in 1990 to 10.6 million in 2000. Even with a much slower rate of growth, the number of American Indians topped the 2 million mark in 2000. These changes caused significant changes in the racial-ethnic composition of the U.S. population. The percentage of Americans who are white decreased from 76 percent in 1990 to 69 percent in 2000. Hispanics made up 13 percent of the population in 2000, up from 9 percent in 1990. Asian Americans rose from 3 percent of the population in 1990 to 4 percent in 2000.

Table 1.1. U.S. Population by Race-Ethnicity, 1990 and 2000

Race-Ethnicity	Population, 1990	Population, 2000	Percent Change	Percent of Total Population, 1990	Percent of Total Population, 2000
White (non-Hispanic)	188,128,296	194,552,774	3	75.6	69.1
Black (non-Hispanic)	29,216,293	33,947,837	16	11.7	12.1
American Indian-Alaska Native (non-Hispanic)	1,793,773	2,068,883	15	0.7	0.7
Asian–Pacific Islander (non-Hispanic)*	6,968,359	10,605,808	52	2.8	3.8
Some other race (non-Hispanic)	249,093	467,770	88	0.1	0.2
Multiracial (non-Hispanic)	NA	4,473,016	NA	NA	1.6
Hispanic or Latino	22,354,059	35,305,818	58	9.0	12.5
Total	248,709,873	281,421,906	13	100.0	100.0

*Includes Asian Americans, Native Hawaiians, other Pacific Islanders, and persons who are both Asian American and Native Hawaiian or other Pacific Islander.

Source: U.S. Census Bureau, Census 2000 Summary File 1. Analysis by author.

Furthermore, in 2000 the U.S. census counted persons identifying themselves as multiracial for the first time. Multiracial persons accounted for 2 percent of the U.S. population in 2000.

State Patterns

As the nation becomes more diverse, higher education policymakers must adapt and be able to offer postsecondary education effectively to a more diverse population of students. However, growth in minority populations between 1990 and 2000 did not occur evenly in the fifty states and the District of Columbia. Analysis of state-by-state demographic changes is necessary to determine the significance of this population shift in various parts of the country.

Although the overall U.S. population increased by 13 percent between 1990 and 2000, the populations of nineteen states grew by more than 13 percent. The ten fastest-growing states were in the West and the South: Nevada (66 percent), Arizona (40 percent), Colorado (31 percent), Utah (30 percent), Idaho (29 percent), Georgia (26 percent), Florida (24 percent), Texas (23 percent), North Carolina (21 percent), and Washington (21 percent).

A smaller total population in some of these states affects the high rate of growth. Among the ten fastest-growing states, only Texas, Florida, and Georgia count among the ten largest states. Although Nevada saw the greatest percentage increase in population, it ranked thirteenth in number of additional persons counted in the 2000 census. California, with an increase of more than 4 million people, saw the biggest number of new residents. In addition to California, seven other states grew by at least 1 million: Texas (3.9 million), Florida (3 million), Georgia (1.7 million), Arizona (1.5 million), North Carolina (1.4 million), Washington (1 million), and Colorado (1 million). Together, these eight states were home to 54 percent of the additional Americans counted in the 2000 census.

Whereas these eight states and several others experienced significant increases in population, seven states grew by under 5 percent: Ohio, Rhode Island, Maine, Connecticut, Pennsylvania, West Virginia, and North Dakota. Yet, despite the low rates of growth, the populations of Ohio and Pennsylvania increased by five hundred thousand and four hundred thousand, respectively. In contrast, three states with growth rates above 5 percent increased in population by less than sixty thousand people: South Dakota, Vermont, and Wyoming.

Hispanics. Not surprisingly, the highest rate of growth among Hispanics occurred in states with small Hispanic populations in 1990. However, the rate of growth among Hispanics was so high across the country that forty-four states saw their numbers increase by more than 40 percent. Led by North Carolina and Arkansas, the Hispanic population more than doubled in twenty-two states located mostly in the South and the

Midwest. The growth of Hispanics in North Carolina far outpaced the rest of the nation. In North Carolina the Hispanic population increased by almost 400 percent. Arkansas and Georgia were the only other states to experience growth among Hispanics of at least 300 percent. Eight states experienced growth between 150 and 300 percent: Tennessee (278 percent), Nevada (217 percent), South Carolina (211 percent), Alabama (208 percent), Kentucky (173 percent), Minnesota (166 percent), Nebraska (155 percent), and Iowa (153 percent). None of these eleven states ranked higher than eighteenth in number of Hispanics in 1990.

The ten states with the largest Hispanic populations in 1990 were not among those with the highest rates of increase. However, many of these states experienced big increases in the number of Hispanics too. The Hispanic populations in Arizona, Colorado, Florida, Illinois, Texas, and New Jersey increased by 50 to 90 percent from 1990 to 2000. In California, the state with the largest number of Hispanics in 1990, the Hispanic population grew by 43 percent. Like California, Massachusetts, New Mexico, and New York were states with large numbers of Hispanics that saw population growth below 50 percent. Although the number of Hispanics increased in many parts of the country, more than 66 percent of the growth in the Hispanic population between 1990 and 2000 occurred in California, Texas, Florida, New York, Illinois, Arizona, and New Jersey.

African Americans. Half of the states were above the national rate of growth for African Americans, which was 16 percent. The African-American population in ten states increased by more than 30 percent: Minnesota (81 percent), Nevada (72 percent), Vermont (56 percent), Idaho (52 percent), Utah (49 percent), South Dakota (44 percent), Arizona (43 percent), Georgia (34 percent), Delaware (34 percent), and Florida (33 percent).

The high rate of increase in the African-American populations of these ten states is partially due to the low number of African Americans living there in 1990. Among the fastest-growing states for African Americans, only Georgia and Florida ranked in the top ten in number of African Americans in 1990. None of the other states with the highest growth rate among African Americans ranked higher than thirty-first in total number of African Americans in 1990.

Whereas states with low numbers of African Americans saw significant increases in that population, states with the largest numbers in 1990 experienced lower rates of growth. From 1990 to 2000, only five states grew by more than 250,000 African Americans: Delaware, Florida, Texas, Maryland, and North Carolina. These five states accounted for 45 percent of the increase in the overall African-American population.

Asian Americans. The Asian American population increased by 50 percent nationally between 1990 and 2000. The largest percentage increases in this population occurred primarily in states with small numbers of Asian Americans in 1990. This population increased by at least 85 percent in ten states: Nevada (175 percent), Georgia (138 percent), North Carolina (130 percent), Minnesota (90 percent), Tennessee (88 percent), Texas (87 percent), Nebraska (87 percent), Arizona (87 percent), Delaware (85 percent), and Florida (85 percent). Of these ten states, only Texas was among the top ten in number of Asian Americans in 1990.

Still, with the exceptions of California and Hawaii, the ten states with the highest numbers of Asian Americans in 1990 experienced growth in this population that was above the U.S. average. For example, New York, the state with the second-largest number of Asian Americans in 1990, experienced a 57 percent increase from 1990 to 2000. Although the number of Asian Americans in California increased by only 40 percent, 10 percentage points below the U.S. average, the 2000 census counted more than one million additional Asian Americans in California.

The states in which this population grew the most were California, New York, Texas, New Jersey, Illinois, Washington, Florida, Virginia, and Georgia, all of which had substantial Asian American populations in 1990. Seventy-five percent of the growth in the U.S. Asian American population occurred in these nine states. California, New York, Texas, and New Jersey alone were home to 55 percent of the additional Asian Americans counted in the 2000 census.

American Indians. The American Indian population grew most rapidly in the South. With the exception of Vermont, the ten states with the greatest increase in numbers of American Indians were in the southern portion of the country: South Carolina (60 percent), West Virginia (46 percent), Kentucky (44 percent), Tennessee (43 percent), Vermont (41 percent), Georgia (40 percent), Louisiana (38 percent), Mississippi (35 percent), Arkansas (35 percent), and Alabama (33 percent).

Most of these ten states had the small numbers of American Indians in 1990. Of the ten states with the largest percentage growth in American Indians, only Louisiana and Alabama were home to more than thirteen thousand American Indians in 1990.

Although none of the states with the largest American Indian populations in 1990 saw the largest percentage growth, about half were above the U.S. average of 15 percent from 1990 to 2000: Texas (30 percent), Florida (29 percent), New Mexico (26 percent), Arizona (23 percent), North Carolina (21 percent), and Montana (17 percent). The increase in the number of American Indians was small compared with other racial-ethnic groups. Between 1990 and 2000, only Arizona and New Mexico populations grew by more than 20,000. Among the ten states with the highest rates of growth, Louisiana had the largest increase (6,590).

Multiracial Individuals. As stated earlier, the 2000 U.S. census allowed people to classify themselves by selecting more than one racial group. The official Census Bureau term is *two or more races,* but this chapter uses the more common term *multiracial.* As with all racial-ethnic categories discussed in this chapter, multiracial applies only to non-Hispanics; multiracial Hispanics are included with all Hispanics. Because multiracial persons were not classified prior to the 2000 census, we are unable to examine the growth of this group during the 1990s. However, because multiracial persons constitute a significant racial-ethnic group it is important to examine their distribution across the country. It is also important to discuss multiracial individuals because they are considered nonwhite; therefore, they add to the population of persons of color in each state.

In 2000, there were 4.5 million multiracial persons in America. Half of them lived in California, New York, Florida, Texas, Washington, Hawaii, and Michigan. California had more multiracial individuals than any other state: 869,052. The largest multiracial ethnicity in California was white and Asian American, accounting for 28 percent of all multiracial persons in the state. Almost 23 percent of multiracial persons in California were white and some other race (*some other race* refers to smaller racial-ethnic groups not included in the categories discussed in this chapter). The state with the second greatest number of multiracial persons was New York, with more than 360,000. The largest multiracial ethnicity in New York was white and some other race. Florida and Texas each had about 230,000 multiracial persons. The largest multiracial ethnicity in Florida was African American and some other race, accounting for 23 percent; in Texas it was white and American Indian, accounting for 25 percent. The largest multiracial ethnicity in any state was white and American Indian in Oklahoma: 73 percent of the nearly 140,000 multiracial persons in Oklahoma said they were white and American Indian.

The Emerging Nonwhite Majority

Growth among racial-ethnic minorities across the country is making some states significantly more racially and ethnically diverse. In 1990, nearly a quarter of all Americans were people of color; by 2000, that percentage had increased 7 percentage points to 31 percent. The percentage of people of color increased the most in Nevada and California, 14 and 11 percentage points, respectively. The percentage of people of color increased by 9 percentage points in Hawaii, and 8 percentage points in seven other states: Texas, New Jersey, Arizona, Washington, Florida, Maryland, and Georgia.

In 1990, Hawaii and the District of Columbia were the only jurisdictions with a majority nonwhite population—69 and 73 percent, respectively. By 2000, New Mexico and California had become majority nonwhite, at 55 and 53 percent, respectively. The growth among people of color in Texas made that state nearly half nonwhite in 2000. Although the percentage of people of color in Mississippi increased by only 2 percentage points from 1990 to 2000, nonwhites made up 39 percent of the state population in 2000. Significant growth in the percentage of people of color in New York, Maryland, and Louisiana made nonwhites 38 percent of the population in all three states. Yet despite the surge in the number of people of color in this country, their percentage in thirty-four states remained below the U.S. average of 31 percent.

The Under-Eighteen Population

It is clear from this analysis of U.S. census data that the diversification of America is occurring unevenly. Although some states are becoming more racially and ethnically diverse, many regions of America remain overwhelmingly white. Yet analysis of the under-eighteen population reveals something different. The racial composition of the under-eighteen population should be of great interest to higher education because this population represents the pipeline of potential students. It is important for higher education administrators and faculty to understand that the youth of America are more racially diverse than the rest of the population. As stated earlier, 31 percent of Americans are people of color. But in 2000, 39 percent of those under the age of eighteen were people of color.

Whereas the total populations in three states and the District of Columbia are majority nonwhite, the under-eighteen populations in four states and the District of Columbia are majority nonwhite: District of Columbia (88 percent), Hawaii (85 percent), New Mexico (68 percent), California (65 percent), and Texas (57 percent).

In seven other states, about half of all persons under age eighteen are not white: Arizona (50 percent), Mississippi (48 percent), Nevada (46 percent), Louisiana (45 percent), New York (45 percent), Florida (45 percent), and Georgia (45 percent). See Figure 1.1.

Even among the states with large percentages of whites, the under-eighteen population shows significant racial and ethnic diversity. Twenty-three states had a total population that was less than 20 percent nonwhite in 2000, but only fifteen states were less than 20 percent nonwhite among persons under age eighteen. West Virginia, New Hampshire, Maine, and Vermont had the smallest percentage of persons of color for all ages. Unlike all other states, these four states did not have significantly more racial and ethnic diversity among persons under eighteen. These are the only states where less than 10 percent of the under-eighteen population is nonwhite.

The under-eighteen population is made up of a variety of racial and ethnic groups in all states, but in several states Hispanics and African Americans account for a particularly large share of the total. Nearly 15 percent of all persons under age eighteen in the United States are African American. In seven southern states and the District of Columbia, African Americans account for over a quarter of the persons under age eighteen: District of Columbia (74 percent), Mississippi (45 percent), Louisiana (40 percent), South Carolina (36 percent), Georgia (34 percent), Maryland (32 percent), Alabama (32 percent), and North Carolina (26 percent).

Whereas 15 percent of Americans under age eighteen are African American, 17 percent are Hispanic. Furthermore, the under-eighteen populations are more than a third Hispanic in four states: New Mexico (51 percent), California (44 percent), Texas (41 percent), and Arizona (36 percent).

Figure 1.1. U.S. Population Under Age Eighteen

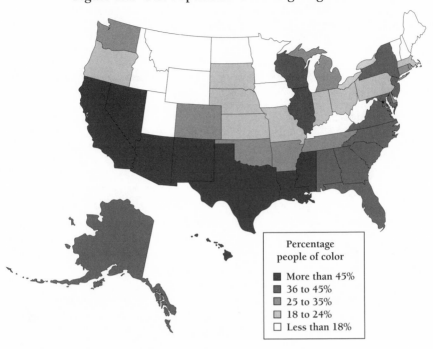

Source: U.S. Census Bureau, 2000. Analysis by author.

Conclusion

Today, the students entering postsecondary education represent America's growing diversity. The population in higher education will become increasingly diverse because the number of people of color in the country is continuing to grow. Although several states remain overwhelmingly white, minorities are expanding their critical mass in many others. In several states minorities are moving toward becoming the majority. The last ten years provide a clear indicator of how America is likely to continue to grow over the next decade. Higher education throughout the nation must be cognizant of these changes. States that have traditionally had few minorities must be prepared to address the educational needs of these students.

In addition to seeing more students of color, colleges and universities will continue to see older Americans from a variety of backgrounds taking advantage of postsecondary education. The success of the local, state, and national economies will depend on the ability of higher education to provide access to students whose age, background, socioeconomic status, and race-ethnicity are varied. These students have different educational goals, learning styles, and attendance patterns. The following chapters in this volume will discuss the needs of these students and the challenges higher education must meet to serve them.

References

Gerald, D. E., and Hussar, W. J. *Projections of Education Statistics to 2012* (NCES 2002–030). Washington, D.C.: U.S. Department of Education, National Center for Education Statistics, 2002.

U.S. Census Bureau. *Census 1990.* [http://factfinder.census.gov/servlet/DatasetMainPage Servlet?_ds_name=DEC_1990_STF1_&_program=DEC&_lang=en]. 1990.

U.S. Census Bureau. *Census 2000* (CD-ROM). 2000.

U.S. Department of Education, National Center for Education Statistics. *Digest of Education Statistics 2001* (NCES 2002–130). Washington, D.C.: Government Printing Office, 2002.

EUGENE L. ANDERSON is a research associate in the Center for Policy Analysis at the American Council on Education.

2

It is increasingly common for students to attend multiple institutions, and this involves more than transfer between institutions. Although sophisticated bureaucratic mechanisms for dealing with course-taking at other institutions have been developed, there is an urgent need to understand its educational implications and to develop ways to enhance educational coherence.

Swirling and Double-Dipping: New Patterns of Student Attendance and Their Implications for Higher Education

Alexander C. McCormick

In the late nineteenth century, colleges and universities began to adopt standardized credit-accounting systems to manage the increasing diversity of students' curricular experiences that resulted from the newly introduced elective system (Levine, 1978). Foundations and national and regional associations advanced standardized criteria for an institution to be considered a college, and this played a role in the further expansion and institutionalization of the credit system. By the turn of the century many institutions recorded course work in standard units and included among degree requirements the accumulation of a certain number of credits. Although it may not have been anticipated, by establishing a curricular currency the standardization movement facilitated equivalency and exchange of course credits—and hence, student mobility—between institutions (Levine, 1978; Cohen, 1998).

For students, portability of credits affords the opportunity to change institutions without sacrificing their progress, to take advantage of unique offerings elsewhere without changing institutions, and more recently, to earn a degree by consolidating work completed at any number of institutions. For institutions, portability of credits dramatically expands the pool of potential students from first-time college entrants to include current students at other institutions and former students who left without a degree. Both private and public institutions seeking to increase enrollment have responded to this broadened market with creativity and vigor by recruiting transfer and reentry students and designing special programs for nonmatriculated students, who receive credit for this work at their "home" institution. This chapter is about the increasingly complex student attendance patterns that result from the portability of course credits and the implications of this complexity for understanding students' educational careers, making judgments about institutional impact, and ensuring the educational coherence of undergraduate programs. This analysis will show that we need far more nuanced ways to think about student careers and to categorize these complex attendance patterns. We may also need to revise policies and practices in light of these patterns.

Why Do Students Attend Multiple Institutions?

Recent years have seen an upsurge in the proportion of students who attend more than one institution. The most familiar form of multiple attendance is one-way transfer; that is, a student completes at least one semester and usually no more than two years of full-time course work (or the equivalent) at one institution—be it a two-year or a four-year institution—and then leaves to complete the degree at a second institution. But there are other patterns of multiple attendance too. Some authors have dubbed them *swirling* (back-and-forth enrollment among two or more institutions) and *double-dipping* (concurrent attendance at two institutions) (de los Santos and Wright, 1990; Gose, 1995). Some swirling and double-dipping students transfer, but others do not: the home institution awards credit for course work completed elsewhere.

Expanding on these notions of swirling and double-dipping, we can hypothesize several possible patterns, many of which emerge from anecdotal accounts:

- *Trial enrollment.* Students experiment with the possibility of transfer to another institution.
- *Special program enrollment.* Students do most course work at the home institution but also take advantage of unique programs offered by others. Examples include the University of Pittsburgh's Semester at Sea, American University's Washington Semester, and Arcadia University's study abroad programs. (According to the Web site of Arcadia University (formerly Beaver College), its more than sixty programs serve eighteen hundred students from 200 colleges and universities (http://www. arcadia.edu/cea/); American University claims that some four hundred students from over 150 institutions participate in its Washington Semester (http://www.american.edu/washingtonsemester/).
- *Supplemental enrollment.* Students enroll at another institution for one or two terms to supplement or accelerate their program. Doing so enables students to take courses not available at the home institution, reduce expenses by enrolling where costs are lower, or make up for a shortfall in credits by enrolling during the summer. Or, there may be purely strategic reasons—for example, a student fearful of earning a low grade in a

required course might complete the course elsewhere; this usually excludes the grade from the transcript and GPA calculations.

- *Rebounding enrollment.* Students alternate enrollment at two (or more!) institutions.
- *Concurrent enrollment (a variation on supplemental or rebounding enroll- ment).* Students take courses at two institutions simultaneously. In addi- tion to the reasons already noted, students may choose concurrent enrollment to expand course availability or scheduling. (In 1995, the *Chronicle of Higher Education* reported that 30 percent of undergraduates at the University of Nevada at Reno and at Arizona State University were simultaneously taking community college courses [Gose, 1995].)
- *Consolidated enrollment.* The degree "program" comprises a collection of courses taken at any number of institutions. In this model, students sat- isfy the awarding institution's residency and other requirements, but a substantial share of their credits come from at least two other institutions.
- *Serial transfer.* Students make one or more intermediate transfers— including reverse transfer from a four-year to a two-year institution—on the way to a final transfer destination. (Serial transfer may be a special case of consolidated enrollment, in which the student follows a relatively linear pattern from one institution to the next.)
- *Independent enrollment.* Students pursue work that is unrelated to their degree program and no credits are transferred (for example, earning com- puter network certification, a real estate license, or other nondegree, often noncredit work).

Many of these categories can be further subdivided by type of institution attended or number of credits involved. Identifying these and possibly other patterns will require careful analysis of enrollment histories, ideally from transcripts, in order to trace the movement of credits between institutions. Adelman (1999a) has taken some initial steps in this direction by identifying and classifying various combinations of institutions attended by students. In his analysis of postsecondary transcripts of 1982 high school graduates, he found that 16 percent of those attending postsecondary institutions followed patterns described here as rebounding or concurrent enrollment, noting that they often combine enrollment at two-year and four-year institutions. These are good first steps, but much remains to be done. The postsecondary tran- script data from the National Educational Longitudinal Study (NELS), con- sisting of 1992 high school graduates, is a promising source for extending and elaborating this type of analysis with more recent data.

What Do We Know About Student Attendance Patterns?

Although it is not a simple matter to gather comprehensive national data on student attendance patterns, several existing sources can shed light on the subject. These include longitudinal studies of high school graduation cohorts, longitudinal studies of new entrants into postsecondary education (regardless of their age at entry), and cross-sectional studies of college graduates. The following paragraphs draw on each of these sources to paint a picture of attendance patterns and what they tell us about how students are finding their way through higher education. The emphasis here is on description rather than explanation.

I begin with the high school cohort studies because these data are the least "fresh"—that is, the most recent study describes the experiences of 1982 high school graduates (at this writing, the newer NELS study already mentioned, describing the experiences of 1992 graduates, is in preparation). These sources also differ from the others because they are based on direct inspection of transcripts collected eleven to twelve years after high school for all study participants known to have continued their education beyond high school, affording a high degree of confidence in the accuracy of the attendance history (Adelman, 1999b). Comparing transcript data for 1972 and 1982 high school graduation cohorts (the National Longitudinal Study of the High School Class of 1972, or NLS-72, and High School and Beyond, or HS&B), Adelman found a marked increase in the proportion of students attending more than one institution (Adelman, 1999a). (It should be noted that Adelman documents the decision rules he used to determine number of institutions attended: graduate-level study was excluded, but attendance during high school or the summer after high school was included; summer-only attendance was always counted in NLS-72 but was counted in HS&B only if a student earned more than six credits in more than two courses; transcript records documenting study abroad, even under the auspices of the home institution, and transcripts requested from foreign institutions were both treated as additional schools in HS&B, affecting 2.8 percent of HS&B college-goers.)

Among students who first enrolled at a four-year institution, the proportion who attended more than one institution increased from 39 to 52 percent; for those who began at a two-year institution it increased from 36 to 47 percent. Limiting the analysis to bachelor's degree recipients, regardless of where they first enrolled, Adelman found that multiple institution attendance rose from about half of the 1972 cohort to about three-fifths of the 1982 cohort. Interestingly, the proportion of bachelor's degree recipients who attended two institutions was relatively stable between the two cohorts (36 to 37 percent); most of the increase came from students attending at least *three* institutions, rising from 13 to 22 percent. Among 1982 high school graduates who went on to complete the bachelor's degree, then, the majority attended at least two institutions and one in five attended at least three. It is important to note as well that this is not just a story about transfer: among 1982 high school graduates who attended two institutions, three in five returned to their first school, as did about half of those who attended three schools.

The foregoing analysis looked in part at attendance patterns of bachelor's degree recipients. Another data source, Baccalaureate and Beyond (B&B), affords a slightly different perspective by sampling students at the time they received the degree. Whereas the previous analyses followed students who finished high school together, we now consider all those who received a bachelor's degree in 1992–93, regardless of when they completed high school (about 70 percent finished high school in 1987 or later). (The data include students for whom the 1993 degree was not their first bachelor's degree, but these have been excluded from the present analysis.) Another important difference from the previous analysis is that these data are based on student interviews rather than transcripts. Adelman's work with the transcript data, in which some transcripts included references to institutions not mentioned by students, suggests that self-reported data likely underrepresent the full extent of multi-institution attendance.

According to the interview data, just over half of 1992–93 bachelor's degree recipients attended more than one undergraduate institution, including about 20 percent who attended at least three institutions. Of those college graduates who began at four-year institutions, 37 percent reported attending more than one institution. Among those who began at a two-year college, 34 percent attended at least three institutions before receiving their degree. As noted previously, this represents more than just transfer between institutions: even among students who graduated from the same institution where they began their college education, one in five had enrolled elsewhere during their college career. (The 37 percent of four-year beginners who attended more than one institution can be broken down into 22 percent who began postsecondary education at a different institution— or transfers—and 15 percent who graduated from the same institution where they began.) Multi-institution attendance was also systematically related to time to degree: those who took longer to complete the degree were more likely to have attended two or more institutions. Even among those who graduated within four years, however, one in three had attended two or more institutions.

Not all students working toward a bachelor's degree complete one, so although examining patterns among bachelor's degree recipients is informative, it provides an incomplete picture. We now turn to recent evidence from two longitudinal studies of first-time college entrants: the Beginning Postsecondary Students, or BPS, studies by the U.S. Department of Education. The first cohort started college in 1989–90 and was last interviewed in 1994; the second started in 1995–96 and was most recently interviewed in 1998. The more recent study thus covers only three years, but the earlier one spans five years since college entry. Although both studies included all new entrants to postsecondary education, the analyses reported here are limited to students who began at two- and four-year institutions and said they were working toward a bachelor's degree. (In the case of the

1989–90 cohort, this excludes two-year students working toward an associate degree who may have had transfer intentions; one-quarter of students at public community colleges indicated they were working toward a bachelor's degree [see McCormick, 1997]. For the 1995–96 cohort, it includes all two-year students with transfer intentions.) Like the B&B results, these data are based on student interviews, so they are equally vulnerable to omissions in enrollment history.

As shown in Table 2.1, about half of new college entrants in 1989–90 who started at a four-year institution enrolled at two or more institutions within five years, one in three having attended two institutions, and 15 percent having attended at least three. The pattern is virtually identical for students who began at public and private four-year institutions. Because their degree objective necessitated transfer, the incidence of multiple attendance was higher among two-year college entrants (63 percent). Because the data for 1995–96 entrants cover only three years, it is not surprising to see less movement among institutions here. Still, 30 percent of those who began at a four-year college and 44 percent of two-year college beginners enrolled at other institutions within the three years; this represents an appreciable number of students and it seems reasonable to expect the numbers will equal or surpass those observed for the earlier cohort.

Table 2.1 also tells us something about the relationship between academic performance and attendance at multiple institutions. GPA comparisons must be approached with caution; norms and standards for grading vary across institutions, departments, and even course sections. Furthermore, the GPA has limitations as a summary measure—for example, we know nothing about the variation in grades across courses, or even about the number of courses used to compute the average. It is nevertheless useful to inquire into the relationship between academic performance and attendance at multiple institutions. One would expect to find higher rates of multiple attendance among students with low grades at the first institution, reflecting academic suspensions as well as voluntary decisions to enroll elsewhere because of academic difficulties (including reverse transfer). The data bear this out: among 1989–90 entrants at four-year colleges, those who attended more than one institution had lower average grades for the first year than those who did not enroll elsewhere. Indeed, attendance at three or more institutions was most common among students with first-year GPAs below 2.25. Nevertheless, even students with strong first-year grades enrolled at other institutions in large numbers, and enrollment at two institutions was common across the range of first-year academic performance. (The relationship with grades appears to manifest itself most strongly at the extremes.)

The picture is different at two-year colleges, where enrollment at a four-year institution signifies goal attainment among students with transfer intentions. Thus, two-year college entrants who attended more than one institution had higher first-year GPAs on average than those whose

Table 2.1. Percentage Distribution of College Entrants Working Toward B.A. Degree, by Number of Institutions Attended[1]

	1989–90 entrants (over five years)			1995–96 entrants (over three years)		
	One	Two	Three or more	One	Two	Three or more
Four-year college entrants						
Total	51.8	33.1	15.1	70.0	25.8	4.2
First institution control						
Public	51.9	33.1	15.0	70.4	25.8	3.8
Private	51.8	32.9	15.4	69.4	25.7	4.9
First-year GPA[2]						
3.25 or higher	57.5	34.4	8.2	76.2	20.5	3.3
2.25–3.24	52.1	32.2	15.7	71.0	24.9	4.1
Below 2.25	45.7	33.5	20.8	61.1	33.7	5.2
Average first-year GPA[2]	2.66	2.55	2.35	(3)	(3)	(3)
Two-year college entrants						
Total	36.8	47.6	15.6	56.0	40.2	3.8
First institution control						
Public	35.4	49.1	15.5	55.7	40.6	3.8
Private	39.2	37.2	23.6	66.7	27.8	5.5
First-year GPA[2]						
3.25 or higher	46.4	39.0	14.6	55.6	40.8	3.5
2.25–3.24	27.0	47.6	25.4	42.6	51.9	5.6
Below 2.25	41.9	44.2	14.0	64.2	33.0	2.9
Average first-year GPA[2]	2.12	2.33	2.56	(3)	(3)	(3)

[1]Student-reported degree goal.

[2]First-year GPA at first institution.

[3]GPA was reported as a categorical variable for 1995–96 entrants.

Source: U.S. Department of Education, National Center for Education Statistics, *Beginning Postsecondary Students Longitudinal Studies: 1989–1994 and 1995–1998,* 1994 and 1998.

enrollment history showed no signs of enrollment at other institutions. These differences do not achieve conventional standards of statistical significance, however.

As suggested earlier, it is important to recognize that attendance at more than one institution is not equivalent to transfer—that is, permanently leaving one institution to continue education elsewhere. The data for the earlier BPS cohort are well-suited to examining the relationship between multiple attendance and transfer because they cover a sufficiently long period to observe transfer behavior, allowing for part-time attendance, stopout, and eventual return to the first institution. (Students were not asked whether they transferred, so transfer is inferred from the attendance history, defined in this case as any transition from the first institution to a second institution without subsequently returning to the first one McCormick, 1997).

Of students who enrolled at more than one institution within five years of college entry, about three out of five transferred (of those who attended two institutions, only about half did). The remainder took courses at other institutions but did not leave their home institution. Students who attended other institutions but did not transfer averaged higher first-year grades than those who transferred (again reflecting, at least in part, students whose academic performance at the first institution was unsatisfactory). More importantly, multiple attenders who did *not* transfer performed comparably in the first year to their counterparts who did not enroll elsewhere.

How Does Multi-Institution Attendance Relate to Persistence and Degree Completion?

This section briefly explores degree and enrollment outcomes for 1989–90 college entrants who were working toward a bachelor's degree. Although Table 2.2 separates those who already earned a bachelor's degree from those still enrolled at a four-year institution, for this discussion the two groups will be considered together as a broad category of students progressing toward the degree. It should also be noted that the last column includes students who completed associate degrees or certificates and students who were enrolled at less-than-four-year institutions, as well as those who will ultimately return to complete the bachelor's degree.

At first glance, it appears that attendance at multiple institutions impaired the progress of students who began at a four-year institution: adding the first two columns of the table, one finds that 76 percent of those attending one institution had completed the degree or were still enrolled in 1994, compared with 65 percent of those attending two or more. But it is not quite so simple, as can be seen when multiple attenders are separated with respect to transfer. Recall that about three out of five multiple attenders transferred; the remainder did not. Among those who attended other institutions but did *not* transfer, the persistence rate was *higher* than among students who attended only one institution (85 versus 76 percent). This finding of high persistence in the case of nontransfer multiple attendance is intriguing, and deserves further study. Only about half of the transfer group persisted, due in part to the presence of reverse transfers and others whose transfer was related to academic difficulty at the first institution. (Previous analysis of these data showed that 45 percent of transfers from four-year institutions were reverse transfers [McCormick, 1997.]) Among those who transferred to another four-year institution, 70 percent had graduated or were still enrolled in 1994.

Although the bachelor's degree persistence rate was lowest among students who transferred from a two-year college, this group includes transfers

Table 2.2. Percentage Distribution of 1989–90 College Entrants Working Toward B.A. Degree, by Degree and Enrollment Status as of 1994

	Attained Bachelor's Degree	Enrolled at a Four-Year Institution	No Bachelor's Degree, Not Enrolled at a Four-Year Institution
All four-year college entrants	55.6	15.0	29.4
Number of institutions attended			
One	63.0	12.6	24.3
Two or more	47.7	17.6	34.7
Four-year college entrants who attended more than one institution but did not transfer	73.0	12.4	14.6
Four-year college entrants who transferred[1]	29.5	21.4	49.2
Transfer destination			
Four-year	42.0	28.5	29.5
All others	11.7	11.3	77.0
Two-year college entrants who transferred[2]	13.4	27.8	58.8
Transfer destination			
Four-year[3]	21.5	44.6	33.8
All others	0.0	0.0	100.0

[1]Includes "reverse" transfers.

[2]Includes transfers to less-than-four-year institutions.

[3]Includes all subsequent enrollment at a four-year institution.

Source: U.S. Department of Education, National Center for Education Statistics, *Beginning Postsecondary Students Longitudinal Study: 1989–1994*, 1994.

to any type of institution and thus does not tell us about the success of students who transferred to four-year institutions. Among two-year college entrants who subsequently enrolled at a four-year institution, the persistence rate was 66 percent, comparable to horizontal transfers from four-year institutions, but with a smaller percentage having completed the degree by 1994 (see Figure 2.1). (See McCormick, 1997, for further analysis of transfer from community colleges.)

The Need for a More Sophisticated Accounting of Attendance Patterns

The preceding analyses show that attendance at multiple institutions is a widespread phenomenon, that it appears to be on the increase, and that it is not limited to transfer between institutions. The rapid expansion of online distance education, the emergence of new "convenience" providers, and the addition of baccalaureate programs at some community colleges all promise to make it even easier for students to enroll at more than one institution,

Figure 2.1. Bachelor's Degree Attainment and Enrollment Status
1989–90 College Entrants as of 1994, by First Institution Type
and Attendance Pattern

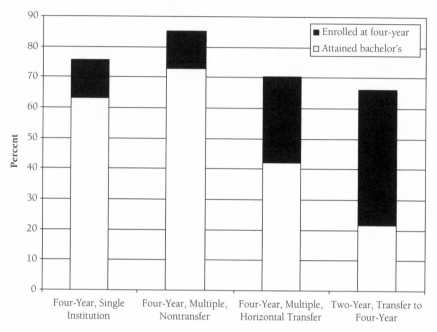

Attendance Pattern (First Institution, Number of Institutions, and Transfer)

Source: U.S. Department of Education, National Center for Education Statistics, *Beginning Postsecondary Students Longitudinal Study: 1989–1994,* 1994.

removing barriers that may have damped mobility in the past. Before we can improve our understanding of the dynamics of multiple institution attendance, we need to develop a more sophisticated understanding of the various ways that students combine enrollment at multiple institutions—one that takes us well beyond simple descriptions of transfer behavior.

In addition to developing a comprehensive framework for analyzing the different manifestations of multiple attendance, we need to understand how it interacts with part- or full-time enrollment status, changes in students' circumstances, and the ways that students finance their education. Most important of all, we need to examine the relationship between multiple attendance and educational outcomes—conceived more broadly than degree completion.

Implications

The increase in multi-institution attendance has far-reaching implications, affecting institutional finances, student financial aid, movements to promote institutional assessment and accountability, research on college impact, student advising, student assessment, and curriculum planning at the departmental and institutional levels.

Approaches to financing public institutions that key funding to student enrollment depend on relatively straightforward and reliable calculations of full-time equivalent enrollment. It is not immediately clear how such systems should take swirling and double-dipping into account. Some institutions may face unexpected shortfalls in tuition revenue as students earn credits elsewhere, whereas others may face unexpected bulges in enrollment demand. Complex patterns of multiple attendance also complicate the assessment of student financial need: the calculation of student budgets presupposes attendance at a single institution during an academic year. As swirling and double-dipping become more common, more students will require exceptional treatment, imposing an additional burden on financial aid offices and complicating the task of planning institutions' financial aid budgets.

When the undergraduate education of half of all bachelor's degree recipients includes experiences in more than one institutional setting—as was the case for 1993 graduates—it is very difficult to make attributions about an institution's educational impact. If educators, policymakers, and researchers are to assess institutional impact, they will need better information about their institution's attendance profile, if not detailed information about the source of credits at the student level, as well as theoretical models that accommodate the complexity of students' attendance patterns. Models that presume uninterrupted single-institution attendance are simply inadequate, except perhaps at a small subset of institutions (and by and large these are not the institutions that are the subject of the accountability agenda).

Most of the patterns hypothesized here—consolidated enrollment being the extreme case—reflect the interplay of two factors: what Schneider and Schoenberg (1999) call "lowest-common-denominator standardization" (and what Adelman [1999a] calls the "postsecondary shopping mall." A sophisticated academic accounting system has grown up around portable course credits and presumed equivalency, facilitating transfer between institutions and students' ability to assemble educational programs from course work at any number of institutions. Whether this accumulation of educational threads amounts to a loose patchwork or a rich tapestry is largely up to the student. The bureaucratic infrastructure that accommodates the portability of course credits has far outpaced the development of frameworks for assessing work at other institutions relative to the broad educational objectives of the institution or the major department. When the only currency is the credit hour, the only question becomes one of course equivalency. Important questions about the coherence and sequence of an educational program go largely unasked. These are conversations that faculty need to have, even in the absence of extensive student mobility between institutions. But mobility makes them all the more urgent. Anecdotal accounts suggest that some students reach their senior year lacking knowledge and skills that faculty expect them to have developed, shortcomings that are sometimes linked to credit for course work at other institutions (and presumed "equivalent") (C. Berheide, personal communication with the author, March 2002).

This calls attention to the importance of academic advising on the one hand and students' academic planning on the other. In Schneider and Schoenberg's words: "Educational goals should not simply be imparted to students; they need to become a continuing framework for students' educational planning, assessments, and self-assessment." They call for a renewed focus on assessments, ideally incorporated into course work, that enable students "to advance, integrate, and correct their understandings at key junctures in their course of study" (1999, p. 35). Another promising avenue is the movement to develop electronic portfolios that document student learning. By whatever means, higher education must confront the educational consequences and imperatives of new patterns of student attendance.

References

Adelman, C. *Answers in the Tool Box: Academic Intensity, Attendance Patterns, and Bachelor's Degree Attainment.* Washington, D.C.: U.S. Department of Education, Office of Educational Research and Improvement, 1999a.

Adelman, C. *The New College Course Map and Transcript Files* (2nd ed.). Washington, D.C.: U.S. Department of Education, Office of Educational Research and Improvement, 1999b.

Cohen, A. M. *The Shaping of American Higher Education.* San Francisco: Jossey-Bass, 1998.

de los Santos, A., Jr., and Wright, I. "Maricopa's Swirling Students: Earning One-Third of Arizona State's Bachelor's Degrees." *Community, Technical, and Junior College Journal,* 1990, *60*(6), 32–34.

Gose, B. "Double Dippers." *Chronicle of Higher Education,* August 4, 1995, p. A27.

Levine, A. *Handbook on Undergraduate Curriculum.* San Francisco: Jossey-Bass, 1978.

McCormick, A. C. *Transfer Behavior Among Beginning Postsecondary Students: 1989–1994.* Washington, D.C.: U.S. Department of Education, National Center for Education Statistics, 1997.

Schneider, C. G., and Schoenberg, R. "Habits Hard to Break: How Persistent Features of Campus Life Frustrate Curricular Reform." *Change,* 1999, *31*(2), 30–35.

U.S. Department of Education, National Center for Education Statistics. *1989–90 Beginning Postsecondary Students Longitudinal Study: 1989–1994,* 1994.

U.S. Department of Education, National Center for Education Statistics. *1989–90 Beginning Postsecondary Students Longitudinal Study: 1995–1998,* 1998.

ALEXANDER C. MCCORMICK *is a senior scholar at The Carnegie Foundation for the Advancement of Teaching in Menlo Park, California.*

Public policy often emphasizes access to higher education, but low-income students face more difficult challenges on the path to degree attainment. Adult low-income students have different obligations and goals than their younger counterparts. Institutional leaders and policymakers can encourage persistence among low-income students with flexible policies that accommodate new enrollment patterns, diverse family structures, and differing educational and economic goals.

Beyond Access: Persistence Challenges and the Diversity of Low-Income Students

Melanie E. Corrigan

This year more than fifteen million students with a variety of educational and personal goals enrolled in institutions of higher education. Demographic projections predict an increase in higher education enrollment to more than seventeen million in 2012 (Gerald and Hussar, 2002). Many of these students will be eighteen to twenty-four-year-olds from low-income families; such students often are people of color, and the first in their families to attend college. In addition, as the economy has taken a downturn in recent years, increasing numbers of older low-income individuals have turned to higher education as a gateway to greater financial stability.

Public policy often emphasizes access to higher education for low-income students, but once in college these students often face the severest challenges on the path to degree attainment. It is through academic success and program completion that students realize the greatest economic benefits of higher education. Institutional choice, financing, work, and attendance strategies are all key components to persistence and success—particularly for the low-income student.

This chapter examines the persistence challenges of low-income students. Because the low-income population is not homogeneous, dependent and independent students will be analyzed separately. Students are defined as *independent* if they are twenty-five years old or older, married, veterans, or have children. *Dependent* students are analyzed based on their total family income, including parental income. In contrast, only the income of the student (and spouse, if applicable) is considered for independent students.

New Directions for Higher Education, no. 121, Spring 2003 © Wiley Periodicals, Inc.

In this analysis, independent students will also be referred to as *adult students*. This chapter also compares low-income dependent students with dependent students from middle- and upper-income families. In general, low-income undergraduates differ from their more affluent peers in several ways: they are more likely to be female, racial or ethnic minorities, older, and supporting a family. Research has shown that, after controlling for student background and other factors likely to affect persistence, low-income students still have lower persistence rates than their more affluent counterparts (Choy, 2000). Family and economic circumstances influence their choice of institution, attendance patterns, and financing options in ways that can negatively affect persistence. Adult low-income students enter higher education with family obligations and economic goals that may vary from their younger counterparts. This chapter will address the impact of these factors on academic success for both of these populations of low-income students.

Besides income, factors such as family structure, attendance status, and living situation influence the financial resources available to undergraduate students. A young undergraduate from a family earning $15,000 per year who attends full-time and lives at home is in a very different financial position than a single mother attending classes part-time and raising two children on a similar salary.

For the purpose of this analysis, low-income students are defined as those with family income equivalent to 150 percent of poverty or less. Poverty thresholds determined by the federal government take into account both income and family structure. For comparison purposes, the analysis of middle- and upper-income families includes families at or above 300 percent of poverty.

In some ways, low-income dependent students resemble higher-income dependent students more closely than independent low-income students. Because of the different challenges faced by dependent versus independent students, this chapter will take a closer look at low-income adults supporting families. Nearly three out of four low-income independent students are supporting dependents. The personal and financial challenges for this group of students are particularly acute and merit such analysis.

Data and Limitations

The data used in this chapter are from several studies conducted by the U.S. Department of Education's National Center for Education Statistics. The National Postsecondary Student Aid Study (NPSAS) provides detailed information on student and family financing of higher education for a single academic year. Beginning Postsecondary Students (BPS) is a longitudinal study that follows first-time beginning students included in the NPSAS studies. The 1998 BPS follow-up tracks students who began three years earlier in 1995–96. Although the limited time frame of the study does not allow for thorough analysis of four-year degree attainment, we can analyze attainment of two-year degrees and interim progress among those students seeking a bachelor's degree.

This chapter focuses exclusively on undergraduate students. Although low-income graduate students also face persistence and attainment barriers, their family and economic circumstances vary widely from those of undergraduates. A thorough analysis of both populations could not be achieved in this chapter. Furthermore, for the most part, the continued academic success of undergraduate students has been the primary concern of policymakers and therefore is the focus of this chapter.

Persistence and Attainment Challenges Among Financially Disadvantaged Students

Given the breadth of financial and academic challenges faced, it is not surprising that low-income undergraduates are less likely to persist and attain a degree than their higher-income counterparts. In 1998, 59 percent of beginning low-income students had either attained a degree or certificate or were still enrolled three years after entry. In contrast, 75 percent of higher-income students had attained or were still enrolled. Many factors contribute to this achievement gap, and low-income students often have multiple risk factors affecting their persistence in postsecondary education (Horn and Premo, 1995). Because these risk factors often are highly intercorrelated, the challenges faced by low-income students are compounded.

This chapter will take a closer look at the impact of these factors: academic background, family circumstances, institutional choice, attendance patterns, and hours worked while enrolled. Different institutional and financing choices of low-income dependent and independent students highlight the improbability of a single set of policies to assist low-income students. In order to help all low-income students achieve and be successful, institutional leaders and policymakers need to create a policy environment that is flexible to the needs of this growing segment of the student population.

Academic Background. Besides financial disadvantages, low-income students often enter higher education with additional risk factors associated with their academic preparation. Students who do not take rigorous high school courses, who earn an alternative high school credential, who delay enrollment, or whose parents did not attend college are less likely to persist through degree attainment (Adelman, 1999). Low-income students are more likely than other undergraduates to possess these risk factors.

As shown in Table 3.1, two-thirds of low-income dependent students come from families in which neither parent attended college, compared with less than one-third of middle- and upper-income students. Conversely, 50 percent of middle- and upper-income students have at least one parent who earned a bachelor's degree or higher, compared with less than 20 percent of low-income dependent students. First-generation students face the disadvantages of less experience and fewer resources for information on the social and academic demands of higher education.

Previous research has shown that students who do not earn a traditional high school diploma and those who delay entry into higher education after high school are less likely to persist and attain than other students (U.S. Department of Education, 1995). Although most entering students have earned a regular high school diploma, low-income students—particularly independents with dependents—are much more likely to have earned an alternative credential. One in five (22 percent) of low-income independent students with dependents had earned an alternative credential compared to 3.3 percent of middle- and upper-income students. In addition, low-income dependent students were much more likely to have delayed entry to postsecondary education after completing high school. Nearly 90 percent of low-income dependent students had delayed entry into college, compared with 24 percent of middle- and upper-income students.

Family Circumstances. Low-income students are more likely than their higher-income counterparts to be independent and support a family. One-third (34 percent) of low-income students are supporting a family, compared with 4 percent of middle- and upper-income students. It is not surprising that most students who are supporting a family also are low-income. However, although one-third of low-income students support a

Table 3.1. Academic Background of Beginning Postsecondary Students, by Income Level, 1995–96

	Low-Income Dependents	Low-Income Independents with Dependents	Middle- and Upper-Income Students
Parents' education:			
High school diploma or less, no postsecondary experience	65.6	59.6	28.1
Some postsecondary experience	19.5	19.2	21.0
Bachelor's degree	11.1	15.6	25.8
Graduate degree	3.9	5.6	25.1
High school completion:			
Traditional diploma	92.6	69.4	94.8
Alternative credential	5.6	21.7	3.3
No high school credential	1.8	8.9	1.9
Delayed entry to higher education	87.6	28.0	23.8
High school curriculum:*			
Not rigorous	51.9	59.8	31.4
Slightly rigorous	28.3	29.7	33.5
Moderately or highly rigorous	19.8	10.5	35.1

*Data available only for students who took the SAT or ACT college admissions exams.

Source: U.S. Department of Education, National Center for Education Statistics, *Beginning Postsecondary Student Longitudinal Study: 1995–1998*, 1998.

family, more than half are dependent. This diversity among the low-income population suggests that a homogeneous approach to support persistence of low-income students will not be effective.

Although many low-income dependent students have family and financial obligations to their parents, they are still more likely to persist than their adult counterparts. Three years after entering postsecondary education, 47 percent of low-income independent students with children had stopped out, compared with 31 percent of low-income dependents. Nearly one-third of all low-income adults had attained a degree or certificate after three years—more than any other group. However, this is largely the result of their disproportionate numbers at two-year and for-profit institutions offering shorter degree and certificate programs.

Institutional Choice. Low-income independents with dependents make different institutional choices than either other low-income students or middle- and upper-income students. Less than 10 percent of low-income independents with dependents attend baccalaureate-granting institutions. Although these students may be more geographically limited in their institutional options than dependent students, they still flock toward shorter-term, often lower-priced, programs in disproportionate numbers. This may suggest, at least in part, that low-income heads of household are choosing these institutions because they are eager to complete their education or training and begin to reap the economic rewards of further education for their family. Shorter academic programs may be more attractive to students with families, who may be returning to school temporarily to enhance their job skills and leave prior to degree attainment if improved employment opportunities materialize.

Low-income dependents, although more likely than independents to attend four-year institutions, still are more likely to attend public two-year and for-profit institutions than middle- and upper-income dependents. Forty-five percent of low-income dependents attend community colleges, compared with 38 percent of middle- and upper-income students. They also are four times more likely to attend two-year and less-than-two-year for-profit institutions (11 percent versus 2.5 percent). Conversely, low-income dependents were less likely than their middle- and upper-income counterparts to attend public or private four-year institutions. Fifty-nine percent of middle- and upper-income dependents began at four-year institutions, compared with 44 percent of low-income dependents.

Low-income dependent students are no more likely than middle- and upper-income dependents to cite financial considerations in choosing their institution. Although academic reasons or varied career goals may be influencing their choices, low-income dependent students are often putting their persistence success at risk by their institutional choices. As noted earlier, low-income students are less likely to persist than middle- and upper-income students regardless of institutional type. However, low-income students attending public two-year institutions and for-profit institutions are at greatest risk for dropping out before attaining a degree or certificate. As shown in Table 3.2, nearly half of all low-income students attending public two-year institutions had not attained a degree and were no longer enrolled in higher education three years after entering, and 38 percent of low-income students enrolled in for-profit institutions had not attained a degree and were no longer enrolled in higher education. This compares with 26 percent and 29 percent of them at public and private four-year institutions, respectively.

Attendance Patterns. Low-income beginning students are more likely to attend part-time than students from middle- and upper-income families. Because part-time enrollment is strongly correlated with type of institution attended—particularly, two-year public institutions—this is not surprising, but it further compounds the persistence challenge for low-income students. Among low-income beginning students, independents supporting dependents were twice as likely as dependent students to attend exclusively part-time. The responsibilities of raising a family may well preclude full-time enrollment and necessitate additional work obligations, but these are both risk factors for continuous enrollment and degree attainment (Pascarella and Terenzini, 1991).

In contrast, the attendance patterns of low-income dependent students more closely resemble those of their middle- and upper-income peers than those of low-income independent students. This disparity between low-income dependent and low-income independent students may suggest that traditional advising and student affairs support services are better suited to the former. With nearly half of low-income heads of households attending

Table 3.2. Persistence and Attainment of 1995–96 Beginning Postsecondary Students, 1998

	Not Enrolled, No Degree	Enrolled, No Degree	Attained Degree or Certificate
All beginning students:	32.3	51.9	15.9
Public four-year	18.8	77.3	3.9
Public two-year	43.6	41.2	15.2
Private four-year	17.2	78.5	4.3
For-profit	34.7	10.1	55.1
Low-income beginning students:	40.9	36.8	22.3
Public four-year	26.1	67.5	6.4
Public two-year	49.1	33.9	17.1
Private four-year	28.8	66.2	5.1
For-profit	38.3	9.5	52.2
Middle- and upper-income beginning students:	25.0	64.8	10.2
Public four-year	15.2	82.1	2.7
Public two-year	38.9	48.0	13.1
Private four-year	11.6	84.6	3.8
For-profit	28.4	11.1	60.5

Source: U.S. Department of Education, National Center for Education Statistics, *Beginning Postsecondary Student Longitudinal Study: 1995–1998*, 1998.

part-time or a mixture of full- and part-time, they have more limited contact with campus services outside the classroom than their traditional age peers. This highlights the importance of easily accessible and comprehensive support services provided on a flexible schedule for adult students.

Interestingly, approximately 56 percent of all part-time students had not attained a degree and were no longer enrolled regardless of income in 1998. However, the complexity of demands on full-time, low-income students resulted in nearly twice as many low-income students stopping out as middle- and upper-income full-time students.

Confounding an analysis of attendance intensity and degree attainment is the emergence of more complex enrollment patterns, including multiple transfers, simultaneous enrollment in multiple institutions, and increased distance education opportunities. Although low-income students are no more likely than middle- and upper-income students to take courses via distance education, beginning postsecondary students attending more than one institution are more likely to be low-income. In Chapter Two of this volume, McCormick details the multitude of new enrollment patterns and their impact on persistence and attainment.

Work. Low-income students, regardless of family structure, are no more likely to work than their middle- and upper-income peers. However, among those students who do work, low-income students work more hours on average (Figure 3.1). Among dependents, 23 percent of low-income students work full-time, compared with 13 percent of higher-income students. Thirty percent of low-income independents supporting a family work full-time in addition to attending classes. Although many low-income students attend part-time while working, the significant number of hours they work contributes to the persistence challenges they face.

Regardless of income, students who worked full-time were less likely to have attained or still be enrolled three years after entering postsecondary education. One-third of beginning postsecondary students working full-time had left postsecondary education without a degree or certificate after three years. However, low-income students working full-time were more likely than middle- and upper-income students to have attained a degree or certificate after three years (29 percent versus 11 percent). Consistent with previous findings, this suggests that low-income working students are concentrated in two-year degree and shorter certificate programs.

Implications and Recommendations

Low-income students face many barriers to persistence and degree attainment, but they do not all face the same challenges. The U.S. Department of Education's National Center for Education Statistics has identified seven risk factors associated with reduced likelihood of persisting through college and earning a degree: being independent, attending part-time, working full-time while enrolled, having dependents, being a single parent, delaying entry to college, and not having a traditional high school diploma.

Figure 3.1. Employment Intensity of Beginning Postsecondary Students, by Income Level and Family Structure

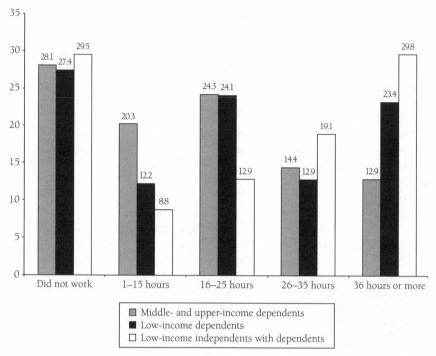

Source: U.S. Department of Education, National Center for Education Statistics, *Beginning Postsecondary Student Longitudinal Study: 1995–1998,* 1998.

Thus, by definition, all independent students have at least one risk factor, and independents with dependents have at least two. Dependent students can have no more than four risk factors (attending part-time, working full-time, delaying entry, and not having a traditional high school diploma). All low-income students have more risk factors than their middle- and upper-income peers. However, low-income adult students face even greater barriers to persistence than low-income dependent students (Table 3.3). In some instances the challenges may be similar, but policies and program development need to address the diversity of the low-income population: What policies and programs are necessary to help *all* low-income students persist and continue to degree attainment?

Chapters Seven and Eight in this volume, by Passaro and colleagues and by Hart, respectively, describe how institutions are designing comprehensive programs to meet the varied needs of low-income students, in particular adult students. Wide-ranging programs integrating academic and financial advising based on an understanding of the myriad personal factors affecting these students help create an environment of success for all students. Chapter Five, by Longanecker and Blanco, highlights the challenge

**Table 3.3. Distribution of 1995–96 Beginning Postsecondary
Students by Income, Dependency, and Number of
Persistence Risk Factors**

	No Risk Factors (%)	One or Two Factors (%)	Three or Four Factors (%)	Five to Seven Factors (%)
All 1995–96 beginning postsecondary students	43.7	30.2	18.2	7.8
Low-income	24.5	32.1	29.7	13.7
Dependents	48.7	46.5	4.9	0.0
Independents with dependents	0.0	2.2	59.6	38.3
Middle- and upper-income	60.3	27.7	9.4	2.6
Dependents	67.1	29.0	3.9	0.0

Source: U.S. Department of Education, National Center for Education Statistics, *Beginning Postsecondary Student Longitudinal Study,* 1998.

of a policy environment that struggles to address the neediest students and consider broader educational success measures. It is no longer reasonable to expect that all undergraduates will attend full-time, limit work, and graduate in four or five years. Particularly for low-income students, family responsibilities and diverse economic and career goals necessitate variable attendance and financing patterns. To serve the needs of these students well, there must be a convergence of sound institutional and governmental policies to encourage persistence through flexible financial aid for new enrollment patterns, institutional support for students' diverse family structures, and targeted academic counseling to the most direct path to reaching a variety of educational and personal goals.

References

Adelman, C. *Answers in the Toolbox: Academic Intensity, Attendance Patterns, and Bachelor's Degree Attainment.* Washington, D.C.: U.S. Department of Education, Office of Educational Research and Improvement, 1999.

Choy, S. *Low-Income Students: Who They Are and How They Pay for Their Education* (NCES 2000–169). Washington, D.C.: U.S. Department of Education, National Center for Education Statistics, 2000.

Gerald, D. E., and Hussar, W. J. *Projections of Education Statistics to 2012* (NCES 2002–030). Washington, D.C.: U.S. Department of Education, National Center for Education Statistics, 2002.

Horn, L. J., and Premo, M. D. *Profile of Undergraduates in U.S. Postsecondary Education Institutions: 1992–93, with an Essay on Undergraduates at Risk* (NCES 96–237). Washington, D.C.: U.S. Department of Education, National Center for Education Statistics, 1995.

Pascarella, E. T., and Terenzini, P. T. *How College Affects Students.* San Francisco: Jossey-Bass, 1991.

U.S. Department of Education. *Descriptive Summary of 1989–90 Beginning Postsecondary Students: Five Years Later with an Essay on Postsecondary Persistence and Attainment.* Washington, D.C.: U.S. Department of Education, National Center for Education Statistics, 1995.

U.S. Department of Education. *Beginning Postsecondary Student Longitudinal Study: 1995–1998.* Washington, D.C.: U.S. Department of Education, National Center for Education Statistics, 1998.

U.S. Department of Education. *National Postsecondary Student Aid Study: 1999–2000.* Washington, D.C.: U.S. Department of Education, National Center for Education Statistics, 2000.

MELANIE E. CORRIGAN is assistant director of the Center for Policy Analysis at the American Council on Education.

4

Productivity strategies such as delegating instruction to computers, minimizing redundant course taking, and the like may not work. To enhance the productivity of today's students, this chapter recommends that institutions take five steps: delineate learning goals, assess student performance, understand how to achieve learning with the particular student population, consider options for increasing productivity, and ensure institutionwide support.

New Modes of Productivity for Student Learning

Barbara E. Walvoord

The challenges facing higher education have been explored in the previous chapters: today's students come from increasingly diverse backgrounds, more are adult learners with specific and diverse goals, learners move among institutions and between face-to-face and distance education, and they often mix education with work, so that they cannot focus exclusively on their education. As students change in these ways, the nation desperately needs educated citizens who possess not just technical skills but also analytic and evaluative skills, integrity, values, creativity, the ability to work with others from diverse backgrounds, flexibility, and openness to change. Stakeholders are demanding that educational institutions demonstrate outcomes. Meanwhile, resources for higher education are increasingly limited. When scarce resources must be used for higher outcomes, the issue is productivity—that is, the ratio of input to output.

Old modes of increasing productivity may not work with the students described in this volume, because their characteristics and attendance patterns change the costs and outcomes. For example, it may not work well to enlarge class size, offer courses on-line, or hire more adjuncts in an attempt to reduce costs for a cohort of students to get their degrees. Such traditional methods of enhancing productivity assume that the diploma itself is sufficient proof of learning. These perspectives view the student as product, not as contributing member of the productivity quotient; they see students as similar, with learning goals in line with the institution's and moving through the institution in cohorts. Finally, such perspectives embrace top-down approaches that do not sufficiently influence the daily actions of faculty and departments, which can significantly affect productivity and

NEW DIRECTIONS FOR HIGHER EDUCATION, no. 121, Spring 2003 © Wiley Periodicals, Inc.

learning. Although old ways of increasing productivity may not work, the characteristics and attendance patterns of these new students offer new possibilities for heightened productivity. For example, they may need fewer services, or different services, than traditional students; they may prioritize convenience of class time and location; and they may be able to learn effectively without traditional classrooms but with a different type of faculty or adviser guidance.

Much of the current work on productivity, even when it recognizes the student characteristics described in this volume, focuses on particular strategies such as delegating some instruction to computers or reducing redundant course taking among students (for example, Johnstone and Maloney, 1998; Massy and Wilger, 1998; Massy and Zemsky, 1995). Yet such strategies may be more or less useful in various situations with different student populations, and more or less achievable in various political environments.

Five Components to Enhance Productivity with Nontraditional Students

If they are to enhance productivity, institutions need to have in place five components; a strategy for enhancing productivity is only one of them. The four other components are goals for learning, measures of the goals, an effective pedagogy, and institutional support.

This program is particularly appropriate for the students described in this volume because it emphasizes multiple points of assessment suited to disparate student learning goals and patterns of attendance; it gives faculty members the best possible opportunity to know their nontraditional students and meet their disparate needs; it ties pedagogy firmly to productivity; it encourages knowledge of the options for pedagogy and productivity; and it emphasizes involvement of faculty and departments.

This chapter explains each of the five components in turn. In each section, an illustration is provided by a 200-level Shakespeare class I taught for sophomore non-majors at the University of Cincinnati, a state research university of thirty-six hundred students. The students in this class exhibited many of the characteristics described in the previous chapters: they tended to be urban commuters from a variety of cultural backgrounds, some in poverty, transfers or about to be transfers, employed more than fifteen hours a week, attending part-time or stopping out, taking courses at other institutions, and facing increasing choices for on-line learning. In that class I tried to increase productivity by handling 40 percent more students (from forty to fifty-six) with no loss of their learning, satisfaction, or retention and less of my own time. A previous publication provides details not possible in this short chapter (Walvoord and Pool, 1998). Here, I show only how the case illustrates the five components.

Goals for Learning. Productivity begins with clear statements of learning goals by both faculty and students. The kinds of students described in this volume may enter higher education with inappropriate or unrealistic goals, or insufficient thought about their goals. Thus, departments and individual faculty should know each student's goals, help to shape those goals, and help students choose strategies to meet their goals.

For the Shakespeare class, I wrote learning goals: "By the end of this class, I would like students to be able to. . . . " (For more examples of goals from various disciplines expressed in this format, see Walvoord and Anderson, 1998.) My most important goals were for students to be able to discuss a Shakespeare play effectively either orally or in a written essay, using the strategies of literary analysis that I taught them in the course; be intellectually creative; take responsibility for their own learning; and reexamine their own ideas and values as a result of reading and discussing the literature. I printed the goals in the syllabus and discussed them thoroughly with students at several points throughout the course.

I also asked students on the first class day to write anonymously for five minutes about their own learning goals, and I read those to see the range of goals and determine whether their goals were consonant with mine. Throughout the course, students kept journals about their progress in achieving their educational goals.

In addition to the learning goals, I also wanted high student satisfaction and a retention rate that was at least as good as other sections of the same course taught by other teachers.

Measures of the Goals. Achieving goals for student learning, satisfaction, and retention in a productive way requires reliable and valid measures, so that individual faculty, students, departments, and institutions have evidence of how well their productivity measures are working, and so that productivity does not mean merely reducing costs to produce a diploma but also investigates quality of learning. Optimally, the measures of learning will be usable by individual faculty and students in classrooms as well as by departments and programs. They will be clear to both students and faculty at the beginning of a course or program, and they will function at various points throughout the educational process. Measures will be transferable among institutions, and they will matter to the faculty, the student, and the institution. Grades are not a sufficient measure of learning unless the criteria and standards for the grades are clear. However, the grading *process* can be used, because it already assesses student learning throughout the curriculum, it reflects faculty members' criteria, and it provides the faculty member and the student with timely indicators of how well their strategies for productivity are working in terms of the learning that is occurring.

In the Shakespeare class, I used several measures for my goals. For the learning goals—especially the skills of written literary analysis—I created a primary-trait scale (Walvoord and Anderson, 1998) that, when used to evaluate the students' essays, allowed me to assess their analytic skills and creativity in a quantifiable, diagnostic way and to share my criteria, standards, and assessments with others. I shared the criteria and standards with the students early in the course. My detailed evaluation of their essays not only informed me about their learning but also contributed to their grades and gave them feedback as I responded to their drafts. Kristen Pool, a graduate student who served as outside observer to the class, also collected the students' perceptions of their own learning through interviews with a selection of them and through journals kept by all of them. We also gathered indirect evidence of student learning through those questions on the national IDEA questionnaire (www.idea.ksu.edu) that deal with student perceptions of their learning. Pool observed and took notes in a number of my class sessions, focusing on such elements as student participation and quality of the discussion.

For a measure of satisfaction, I used the student interviews that Pool conducted as well as the IDEA questions that dealt with satisfaction. For retention, I compared the number of students who dropped my class with those from the eighteen other sections of the same course taught that semester by other teachers.

Pool's time was a resource that enabled fuller gathering of evidence. However, I have worked with hundreds of faculty who have assessed student learning without the help of a graduate student, using their own grading processes, student evaluations, and as they had time, other data such as student questionnaires or journals. The point is that with the populations of students described in this volume, learning must be assessed often throughout the curriculum to inform faculty and departments about how their strategies for productivity are working. The least costly and often most reliable way to assess student learning is through classroom work that is thoughtfully assigned, systematically assessed by clear criteria and standards, intelligently used to inform classroom teaching, and then shared with colleagues for departmental or programmatic decision making.

Effective Pedagogy. It does not help to know that your students are not performing as well as you would hope unless you also have some idea of what strategies might help them learn better. This requires knowledge of educational research and also the faculty's and the students' own observation of and reflection on their learning.

Traditional educational research provides some indications about how higher learning goals can best be achieved (for example, Astin, 1993, 1996; Chickering and Gamson, 1987; Pascarella and Terenzini, 1991; Levin and Kosky, 1998). That literature emphasizes the importance of student involvement and classroom interaction with teachers and peers. Much of it assumes traditional student age and demographics. New research and theory are needed as student populations and attendance patterns change.

Understanding how to achieve learning also requires faculty and departments systematically to observe and reflect on their *own* students' characteristics, institutional and student cultures, learning processes, and outcomes—data that the local faculty and departments have requested, know well, and can use to improve productivity and learning. (Useful guides for faculty and departments include Angelo and Cross, 1993; Banta, Lund, Black, and Oblander, 1996; Brookfield, 1995; Nichols, 1995a, 1995b, 1995c; Tierney, 1990; Walvoord and Anderson, 1998. See also Flashlight program at www.TLTGroup.org.)

The literature—as well as my own experience directing faculty development projects and coaching individual faculty about their teaching at many different kinds of institutions—suggests that the following teaching strategies are particularly important to the kinds of students described in this volume. These are presented here simply as a list; to explain further or to offer examples is beyond the scope of this chapter. However, the description of the Shakespeare class, following the next component description, illustrates how one teacher implemented these pedagogies.

- Gather and use rich information about each student's background, learning goals, learning style, and culture. Do not assume that all students are the same.
- Set high standards for student achievement, and help students set high standards for themselves.
- Clarify time requirements; emphasize that being educated requires time, that time-on-task is one of the most powerful predictors of learning, and that college requires a different ratio of class time to study time than high school.
- Assess student learning, satisfaction, and retention. Use your own class assignments, tests, and exams, as well as student evaluations and questionnaires, to assess student classroom work.
- Give frequent feedback to students throughout the learning process.
- Help students manage their time constraints. Try to manage the learning process so as to waste as little of their time as possible, help them learn to study efficiently, and insofar as your time allows, or in collaboration with others, help students make good decisions about employment hours, travel, budgeting, and extracurricular involvement.
- Respect and use students' own knowledge, skills, and learning styles.
- Introduce students to the culture of higher education by providing explicit cultural information.
- Attend to issues of self-image, identity, and attribution. Help students envision themselves as proactive learners, professionals in training, rather than as passive students doing just enough to get the grade. Help them attribute their successes and failures to their own efforts and decisions, rather than to luck, teacher-didn't-like-me, or other attributions that rob them of power to change.
- Help students engage with each other in meaningful academic tasks.
- Provide students with as much access as possible to you and to each other, even when they are in different locations at different times.

Productivity in Achieving the Goals. Faculty, students, and administrators need to know the strategies that can increase productivity and how those strategies may affect the kinds of students described in this volume. As I have said earlier, much of the literature on productivity suggests specific strategies for increasing productivity. With the four following productivity strategies, I have tried to derive the principles that lie behind such lists and to focus on classroom techniques that can be used by faculty and departments in traditional institutions. The examples at the end of the chapter illustrate some ways to implement these four strategies.

Provide High-Cost Services Just at Point of Need. High-cost services such as individual response to student work and individual or small-group interaction with a faculty member are powerful learning tools extremely valuable to all students, but especially to those described in this volume. Such services must be provided richly and quickly at points of need to students who are ready to benefit. However, these services should not be used when less expensive methods could achieve the same results. They should not be given to students who do not need the help or are not ready to benefit.

Extend the Usefulness of Resources While Reducing Their Cost. Increase the number of students who can make use of a single faculty or expert utterance or resource. For example, use interactive video for distant students so more students can listen to a lecture or demonstration. Make sure your resources are in the most effective form and medium for learning. It does not matter how many students listen to a lecture if the lecture does not help their learning. Consider also the cost of the resource for both institution and student. A student who has to go to the library or her workplace to access the Web may be better served by a printed syllabus she can keep on her desk at home.

Delegate. Use high-paid faculty for what only faculty can do. When possible and productive, delegate other tasks to computers; to adjuncts, staff, or graduate students; or to students themselves, helping them take responsibility for their learning.

Help Students Be Productive. Help students make the best use of their own time and the best decisions. Help them with productive study habits; when possible, structure class meetings and locations to save them travel time; guide them in decision making about employment outside of school, attendance, choice of institution, choice of distance or face-to-face instruction, and the like. *Opportunity cost* and *productivity* are concepts every student should understand.

The Shakespeare class provides a good example of how one faculty member implemented both the pedagogical principles and the strategies for productivity described in the preceding paragraphs. As noted, the class was one of nineteen sections that quarter of a 200-level sophomore literature class required of many University of Cincinnati students as part of their general education. Traditionally, the English department had resisted the form of productivity that many other departments used for sophomore non-majors courses: extending the "reach" of a lecture by running large lecture classes of several hundred students with graduate students as graders and perhaps discussion leaders or lab supervisors (although some large courses did not have discussion sections or labs). Instead, the department had placed great emphasis on capping these sophomore sections at forty-five students each in order to preserve what were believed to be important factors in learning: class discussion, teacher response to writing, and a sense of community in the classroom, where the teacher knows each student and students know each other. But the system had several unproductive elements. First, most classrooms were arranged in rows, and forty-five is a large number of students for effective discussion. If you walked the halls of the main classroom building in the middle of the day, you would see many of these classes being taught by lecture with little student engagement. Furthermore, at a research university it is difficult for faculty to find the time to grade batches of forty-five papers, especially from non-majors, so there was less response to student writing than our departmental ideals and theories would suggest.

However, even if I did my best to encourage discussion and spent lots of time responding to student papers, I still envisioned a teaching scene that had many unproductive elements. Most students in the class would be employed for fifteen, twenty, even thirty or forty hours a week. I knew that if I met them as a group in the bolted-seats, raked-row lecture classroom assigned to me, it would be hard to involve even half of them on any given day. Most students would not read the plays until after I had lectured; many would not read the plays at all but would rely on *Cliff Notes* and their class notes. Many would write the papers in a single night with questionable use of Web sources. I would be violating the productivity principles listed earlier by using my faculty time to present information that could have been delegated to reading and offering individual feedback to student work that did not represent enough of the student's investment to merit my high-cost time. Meanwhile, I was maintaining a demanding publication schedule, and I wanted to reduce my teaching time if I could do so with no diminution of student learning, satisfaction, or retention.

Another productivity issue was that our departmental capping policy, combined with loss of faculty positions and other demands on faculty time, meant that there were not enough sections for the demand. Students were coming frantically to my office during registration week, saying, "I've tried three times to get into a lit class, which I need to graduate, and each time there was no room. Please let me in; I'll sit on the floor." I was disturbed by the hardships we were creating for students and wanted, if possible, to help the department address these issues.

The first thing I did was to rethink the use of the most costly item in the productivity equation: my own time. Attending as well to the learning side of the productivity equation, I also placed high priority on the pedagogical strategies I knew were effective with the type of students in my class: active learning where students themselves must talk and write about the literature they have read, frequent feedback on their work, accountability for class preparation, a teacher who knows their names and their work, and engagement with peers in meaningful intellectual tasks.

I decided not to lecture at all, but rather to delegate the delivery of information and ideas to readings and to videotaped lectures on Shakespeare's plays that my library owned or could purchase. I also wanted to help my students make better use of their own time, minimizing the driving, parking, babysitters, and other costs to them of class attendance—costs that were of questionable value if they merely sat silent for the whole hour. Students could watch the videotaped lectures and read the material on their own time in their own spaces. Obviously, for some classes and disciplines, and with students who had access to computers, interactive learning software could be used.

I wanted to use my time not to deliver information but to engage in discussion with students and respond to their writing, encouraging their development of sophisticated analytical skills and creativity. These were the most difficult aspects of teaching. They could not be delegated to computers, student peers, or teaching assistants. I was trying to use my time to do what only I could do. I decided that it was better for students to meet for discussion an hour a week with a group of about fifteen, where discussion could be very lively and everyone was expected to participate, rather than three times a week in a room of forty to forty-five students seated in fixed rows, where it would be difficult for me to engage them or hold them accountable for thoughtful reading. I wanted to place as great a value on their time as on my own, ensuring that if they arranged their work schedule or hired a babysitter, drove all the way across town, cruised for a parking space, and trekked a thirty-pound backpack to my classroom, it would be well worth their while.

So I rearranged time, space, and roles for greater productivity. Each week, students would do these things: (1) read the play assigned for that week, as well as any other assigned reading, (2) listen to two videotaped lectures about the play (these were on reserve in the library, and some were broadcast on the campus TV station), (3) write a one- to two-page analysis of an aspect of the play, (4) keep a journal about their learning progress, and (5) attend one class session of fifty minutes, where they would meet with me and a total of some fourteen other students for discussion. Following the pedagogical principles listed earlier, my standards were high and accountability was strict. To this class discussion session students were required to bring their notes on the play, a text of the play, notes on the taped lecture and other readings, and the short written assignment ready to hand in. During the class, they would be responsible for talking from their written assignment, demonstrating familiarity with the play and assigned readings, expanding their own insights, helping other students to think more deeply, and taking notes on the discussion. An extensive handout from me helped them learn effective discussion strategies—part of their training in academic culture. Each student would be graded on her participation in class. They would all complete a self-assessment questionnaire at the end of the class session, aimed at helping them and me to assess how they were meeting their learning goals. Twice during the ten-week quarter they would write a five- to eight-page formal essay.

I spent my time each week in the following way: one hour to create a one- to two-page assignment about the play and six hours meeting with each of six small discussion groups in small rooms that the registrar had made available to me at various times of the day. I did not take home the short weekly papers because I responded to them in class. I did take home and respond to drafts and final copies of the first formal essay, as well as the final copy of the last essay, which served as the final exam. Prior to the semester, I previewed and purchased the videotaped lectures and set them up for student borrowing in the library. I figured that I spent three hours less per week than if I had taught the class by the lecture method (specific time allocations are presented in Walvoord and Pool, 1998).

In other words, I was able to handle more students in less time while implementing sound pedagogy for learning: ensuring that every student spoke in class at each weekly session, wrote every week and received a response, received a draft response to his analytic essays, and participated in a learning community where he was known by me and his classmates. The quality of their learning was high, as judged by Pool's and my systematic analysis of their papers and by their course grades. Pool's interviews with class members, as well as the IDEA questionnaire and students' journals, indicated that they highly valued the pedagogical strategies and course structure. They reported that they learned well and especially appreciated the opportunity to come to class only once a week (specific results are reported in Walvoord and Pool, 1998). In effect, I had created for them a kind of "distance" course where they could do more work on their own and attend class less frequently. For example, one student said in an interview, "It wasn't like, 'Oh, we're only meeting once a week, this is cake.' We were doing the full load. I'd go watch the videos on Monday, write my logs and then write my assignment, and go to class on Wednesday. . . . It wasn't like, 'Oh no, this is too much.' It was evened out. It was put together extremely well. You taught yourself" (Walvoord and Pool, 1998, p. 45). The drop rate was exactly the same as the average of the eighteen other sections of the same course being taught that semester.

The pedagogical strategies used in the Shakespeare class are especially useful for the students described in this volume. I eased their problems of transportation, parking, and travel time by reducing direct contact in class and making that contact very intensive for maximum learning. They could get basic information and an interpretive framework for the plays through the taped lectures, which they could view with greater flexibility. I held them strictly accountable each week for reading and writing, and I gave them weekly feedback. I made explicit the standards for student work and the underlying cultural assumptions about how to conduct themselves in a college-level discussion class. I helped them form their learning goals and monitor their own progress. I helped them make meaningful contact with other students and engage with their peers, thus satisfying their need for community.

To increase productivity, I used the strategies mentioned earlier: I provided small group discussion and individual response to drafts of papers at points when students were attentive and ready to benefit. I spent my time in these intensive interactions and delegated to videotapes the presentation of basic information and analysis. I extended the reach of these taped lectures by making them available for loan in the library and by broadcasting them on campus TV. I delegated to students appropriate responsibility for their own learning. They were in class fewer hours but responsible for more hours of study on their own. I helped them make productive use of their time.

Institutional Structures. The Shakespeare class illustrates what a motivated teacher can do on her own with departmental support that she requests from sympathetic colleagues and administrators. For the Shakespeare class, the department chair and the director of undergraduate studies were highly supportive, encouraging me and assigning Kristen Pool to help me gather data during the trial semester. However, these were local, situation-specific adjustments made for a single faculty member at her request. To enhance productivity throughout an institution more robust institutional structures are required. Two basic approaches are possible: radical restructuring of the educational process in nontraditional institutions, and new strategies within traditional structures. These approaches are not mutually exclusive; traditional institutions usually adopt and modify experiments first initiated in nontraditional settings.

Examples of Radical Institutional Restructuring. Nontraditional programs radically disaggregate and restructure faculty and institutional roles, helping even traditional institutions to think creatively. An example is The Union Institute & University, which offers baccalaureate, master's, and doctoral programs to its three thousand adult students, about one-third of them minority. Based on the medieval Oxford model with its individual tutors, and on the theories of John Dewey, UI&U is learner-centered, learner-designed and paced, and multidisciplinary. Every degree is individualized, with emphasis on the learner's contribution to society. Rather than follow a traditional framework of courses and credits, learners work with faculty mentors to define their own paths of inquiry as well as the standards by which their work will be evaluated by their own mentors and by other members of the faculty (see www.tui.edu).

UI&U addresses productivity by focusing its resources on providing the most costly yet often the most powerful aspect of education—individual faculty mentoring and evaluation—while reducing other costs, such as traditional classroom and credit structures. Because mentoring is individual, faculty can concentrate the most time on learners who need the most guidance, which helps limit this high-cost mentoring to those situations where it can really be effective. UI&U also employs peer interaction for learners.

The Western Governors University requires no credits or class attendance, and it does not itself offer any instruction (www.wgu.edu). Instead, it focuses its resources on assessment of student learning. Students must demonstrate their mastery of the required competencies: they take standardized exams, write papers, produce research projects, and in some fields, demonstrate workplace competence. Unlike UI&U, where assessment, like mentoring, is individualized, assessment at WGU is standardized: all students in a degree program take the same tests for the same competencies as well as general-education competencies common to many degree programs. Students are guided by adviser-mentors. The adviser-mentor helps the student assess what competencies she already has and what competencies she needs to acquire by individual study or by enrolling in courses offered at other institutions. WGU enrolls students from around the world, using technology to enhance adviser-student communication and facilitate assessment. Some students take courses on-line from various institutions. Whereas the emphasis at UI&U is on intensive engagement with faculty mentors and individualized inquiry, the emphasis at WGU is on demonstrating competencies that are the same for every learner in a program. Both institutions disaggregate and rebalance traditional faculty and institutional roles in ways that can help us think outside traditional boundaries.

The University of Phoenix, unlike UI&U and WGU, operates with credits and classes, but reduces the costs of those structures (www.phoenix.edu). To teach its courses, it hires adjuncts who are practicing professionals in their fields, and it provides those faculty with standardized course plans. It saves students time by holding classes at convenient times and locations, usually near major highways or malls. Students may also take courses on-line; lectures, questions, and other materials are delivered on-line, and faculty act as guides to learning. In the on-line version, faculty spend less time delivering lectures and more time responding to individual students.

These three nontraditional institutions balance each other in provocative ways, each using its resources differently to emphasize different aspects of the educational process, each defining in different ways the roles of faculty, advisers, and students.

Examples from Traditional Institutions. At traditional institutions facing the student characteristics and attendance patterns described in this volume, greater productivity must be achieved inside the feasible boundaries of course and credit structures, academic departments, and faculty roles. Two approaches to productivity predominate: focusing institutionwide efforts on specific measures to improve productivity, and providing incentives and support for faculty and departments to enhance productivity in their own spheres.

An example of the first approach—institutionwide efforts—is Mercy College, described by Passaro and her colleagues in Chapter Seven of this volume. Mercy College identified student retention and student learning as aspects that could improve its productivity. After curricular reform failed to show significant improvement in student retention, the college turned to a much broader, institutionwide effort. This includes not only curriculum but also marketing, recruitment of students, and financial aid—all aimed at recruiting more highly motivated students with a better chance of succeeding—and then providing those students with a thoughtful curriculum as well as support structures that facilitate success and yet are affordable. This school's story illustrates institutionwide efforts focused on a specific strategy for productivity: increasing retention and improving learning.

A second approach for traditional institutions has been to provide incentives and support for faculty and departments to achieve greater productivity in their own spheres, using their own ingenuity. Because faculty and departments have high autonomy, their individual decisions about time allocation, teaching load, use of adjuncts and teaching assistants, course structure, teaching methods, and curriculum significantly affect an institution's productivity (Levin and Kosky, 1998). Also, their autonomy makes it difficult to organize them into a tight, hierarchical structure around institutionwide programs. But autonomy encourages local ingenuity and problem solving. Thus, one approach is to build on that strength, encouraging faculty and departments to find their own ways to enhance productivity. A key question, however, is whether to let faculty and departments use any means they choose or to limit them in some way. The two following examples have relied on incentives for faculty or departmental initiatives but have chosen two different ways to limit that freedom.

Worcester Polytechnic Institute, in Worcester, Massachusetts, received funding from the Davis Foundation for eleven faculty in seven departments to experiment with instructional designs intended to increase productivity in introductory courses such as science, mathematics, engineering, and drama. The grant stipulated that the course should include cooperative learning facilitated by upper-class learning assistants. In this way, WPI dictated a pedagogical strategy that some research has shown to be effective for learning. Faculty members were not allowed to achieve productivity in any way that seemed good to them but instead had to incorporate the required pedagogy. Another limit on faculty and departments was a strict accountability and assessment requirement: faculty submitted data on their course costs and outcomes, and the institution supported development of accounting models to determine productivity (Catterall, 1998).

The Pew Grant Program in Course Redesign has supported cohorts of ten institutions a year, each to restructure a large introductory course. There is no requirement for a certain pedagogy, as at WPI. However, institutions that enter the program are supported by extensive guidance for faculty and departments in redesigning courses and in measuring productivity, including measures of outcomes such as learning and retention (Center for Academic Transformation, 2001). Through this guidance, the program exerts some centralized influence over faculty and departmental entrepreneurship. The projects have demonstrated significant savings as well as enhanced learning outcomes.

Both of these approaches for traditional institutions—a centralized effort aimed at a particular productivity strategy such as retention, and incentives for faculty and departmental ingenuity—have strengths and drawbacks that will play differently in different situations. They are not mutually exclusive, but could be combined in different ways depending on institutional culture. Both approaches need the context of the five components described in this chapter. Mercy College has had all of them in place, as have the WPI and Pew programs.

Implications for the Future

Most of the literature on productivity concerns specific measures for achieving it—delegating instruction to computers, minimizing redundant course taking, and the like. But such strategies may not work well with the kinds of students described in this volume, and they may be more or less politically or economically feasible in different environments. To help institutions choose among these strategies and make them work, this chapter has recommended that they have in place five components: learning goals, measures of student performance, knowledge of how to achieve learning with the particular student population, knowledge of options for increasing productivity, and institutionwide support. The story of the Shakespeare class illustrates how productivity may be enhanced, even in humanities classes, by thoughtful application of the first four components. However, enhancing productivity throughout an institution requires broader institutional supports. Nontraditional institutions help us think in new ways about institutional productivity because they disaggregate faculty roles and rearrange educational components. Traditional institutions may focus a coordinated institutionwide effort on a particular productivity goal, such as retention, as Mercy College has, or they may provide incentives and support for faculty and departmental initiatives.

The new students described in this volume change the game for achieving productivity. To accommodate these students and to find ways of enhancing productivity in their own specific environment, institutions should not merely employ top-down strategies that they believe will enhance productivity. Instead, they must ensure that all five components are firmly in place. Doing so allows an institution to choose among various strategies for enhancing productivity, to tailor those strategies to its local situation and goals, to discover whether its productivity measures are effective, to focus on student learning as the sine qua non of educational productivity, and to generate creative solutions for the productivity dilemmas and possibilities that future students will present. Such steps are central to the future of a nation that desperately needs educated citizens from all backgrounds who possess not merely technical skills but real wisdom, and who are educated in ways that most efficiently employ our limited resources.

References

Angelo, T. A., and Cross, K. P. *Classroom Assessment Techniques: A Handbook for College Teachers.* (2nd ed.) San Francisco: Jossey-Bass, 1993.

Astin, A. W. *What Matters in College: Four Critical Years Revisited.* San Francisco: Jossey-Bass, 1993.

Astin, A. W. "Involvement in Learning Revisited: Lessons We Have Learned." *Journal of College Student Development,* 1996, 37(2), 123–134.

Banta, T. W., Lund, J. P., Black, K. E., and Oblander, F. W. *Assessment in Practice.* San Francisco: Jossey-Bass, 1996.

Brookfield, S. D. *Becoming a Critically Reflective Teacher.* San Francisco: Jossey-Bass, 1995.

Catterall, J. S. "A Cost-Effectiveness Model for the Assessment of Educational Productivity." In J. E. Groccia and J. E. Miller (eds.), *Enhancing Productivity: Administrative, Instructional, and Technological Strategies.* New Directions for Higher Education, no. 103. San Francisco: Jossey-Bass, 1998.

Center for Academic Transformation. [http://www.center.rpi.edu], 2001.

Chickering, A. W., and Gamson, Z. F. "Seven Principles for Good Practice in Undergraduate Education." *AAHE Bulletin,* 1987, 39(7), 3–7.

Johnstone, D. B., and Maloney, P. A. "Enhancing the Productivity of Learning: Curricular Implications." In J. E. Groccia and J. E. Miller (eds.), *Enhancing Productivity: Administrative, Instructional, and Technological Strategies.* New Directions for Higher Education, no. 103. San Francisco: Jossey-Bass, 1998.

Levin, H. M., and Kosky, W. S. "Administrative Approaches to Educational Productivity." In J. E. Groccia and J. E. Miller (eds.), *Enhancing Productivity: Administrative, Instructional, and Technological Strategies.* New Directions for Higher Education, no. 103. San Francisco: Jossey-Bass, 1998.

Massy, W. F., and Wilger, A. K. "Technology's Contribution to Higher Education Productivity." In J. E. Groccia and J. E. Miller (eds.), *Enhancing Productivity: Administrative, Instructional, and Technological Strategies.* New Directions for Higher Education, no. 103. San Francisco: Jossey-Bass, 1998.

Massy, W. F., and Zemsky, R. *Using Information Technology to Enhance Academic Productivity.* Washington, D.C.: Educom, 1995.

Nichols, J. O. *Assessment Case Studies: Common Issues in Implementation with Various Campus Approaches to Resolution.* Edison, N.J.: Agathon Press, 1995a.

Nichols, J. O. *Departmental Guide and Record Book for Student Outcomes Assessment and Institutional Effectiveness.* Edison, N.J.: Agathon Press, 1995b.

Nichols, J. O. *A Practitioner's Handbook for Institutional Effectiveness and Student Outcomes Assessment Implementation.* (3rd ed.) Edison, N.J.: Agathon Press, 1995c.

Pascarella, E. T., and Terenzini, P. T. *How College Affects Students.* San Francisco: Jossey-Bass, 1991.

Tierney, W. G. (ed.). *Assessing Academic Climates and Cultures.* New Directions for Institutional Research, no. 68. San Francisco: Jossey-Bass, 1990.

Walvoord, B. E., and Anderson, V. J. *Effective Grading: A Tool for Learning and Assessment.* San Francisco: Jossey-Bass, 1998.
Walvoord, B. E., and Pool, K. J. "Enhancing Pedagogical Productivity." In J. E. Groccia and J. E. Miller (eds.), *Enhancing Productivity: Administrative, Instructional, and Technological Strategies.* New Directions for Higher Education, no. 103. San Francisco: Jossey-Bass, 1998.

BARBARA E. WALVOORD is coordinator for the North Central Association Accreditation Self-Study, and former director of the Kaneb Center for Teaching and Learning at the University of Notre Dame.

5

Public policy is likely to remain more reactive than proactive, and more iterative than creative, in responding to the needs and concerns of students with new attendance patterns. Swirling students will likely swirl even more among institutions, but it will take some time before our policies catch up.

Public Policy Implications of Changing Student Attendance Patterns

David A. Longanecker, Cheryl D. Blanco

Public policy addresses public concerns in four ways. First, it funds and provides programs or services, such as public institutions of higher education at the state level, or the Pell grant program at the federal level. Second, it essentially contracts with independent entities for the desired service, as some states do through private college contracts and the federal government does through programs such as grants for scientific research. Third, the government may act as a catalyst, providing incentives to provoke action consistent with the desired public issue, through state and federal "innovation funding"; the Fund for the Improvement of Postsecondary Education (FIPSE) is an example of this. Fourth, the government may mandate actions by others through laws and regulations that lead to the desired public outcome.

This chapter examines public policy's response to changing student attendance patterns. We start with a look at past and present policies of the four types described and finish with a discussion of future public policies, examining how they need to change to respond effectively to changing attendance patterns. We also examine whether government has the capacity to support such changes.

Public Policy Response

Previous chapters have shown how changes in the social, political, and economic environment have stimulated gradual changes in student attendance patterns. Those incremental shifts in the ways students attend college have become more discernible in the past decade, until nontraditional patterns

NEW DIRECTIONS FOR HIGHER EDUCATION, no. 121, Spring 2003 © Wiley Periodicals, Inc.

now approach the norm. A quick review of how these environmental changes relate to higher education public policy will help set the stage for a more in-depth discussion of the ways in which policy influences attendance patterns.

How We Got Here. Derek Bok (1986) noted that autonomy has been one of the distinguishing features of American higher education institutions. Freedom from government control has encouraged tremendous growth in the numbers and types of postsecondary institutions, allowing faculty wide latitude in hiring personnel and designing curricula, and permitting institutions to acquire funds from a variety of sources. That autonomy has shaped the ways in which colleges and universities interact with their students as well. Throughout most of the history of American higher education, institutions—acting individually or collectively in systems—operated under the premise that they knew best what kind of educational experience students should have. This paternalistic approach did not encourage students to change; mom and dad were simply replaced with a somewhat larger group of adults who would shepherd them through the next four or five years of their lives. Residency requirements and in loco parentis–type policies allowed institutions to exert strong control over students, fostering neither mobility nor independence.

Until recently, the preponderance of college students were traditional age dependents. This large, relatively homogeneous pool of recent high school graduates made it fairly easy for higher education to maintain the status quo, because these students all wanted much the same experience. Only a small proportion of enrollments through the 1960s fell outside this norm in age or educational motivation, and those who were nontraditional looked to community colleges and proprietary schools, rather than to comprehensive four-year public or private institutions, for their higher education opportunity.

But the phenomenal demographic and social transformations of recent decades have changed forever college students and their expectations. To open college doors to all who can benefit, and to achieve a level of social mobility that creates a rich and genuinely diverse culture, people from all corners of American life—educators, parents, businesspeople, policymakers, and others—have worked hard. Students have taken this opportunity seriously and are now defining the college experience in terms of their life goals in very different ways: they may be looking for a few courses or a subset of an academic program rather than a degree; they may not be willing to have their higher education experience limited by the space and time boundaries set by traditional colleges and universities; they may care little about finding those experiences in a single institution over a four-year period. In sum, the paternalistic environment that institutions thrived on does not work for the student of today.

On the political front, the influence of policymakers and new state governance structures on higher education has grown. The expansion of statewide coordinating and governing boards that began in the 1970s was accompanied by a shift in authority over policies relating to students and how they moved in and out of colleges and universities. Likewise, lawmakers have become active overseers of public (and to some extent private) institutions. The rise of accountability as a policy goal in the late 1980s and early 1990s signaled policymakers' increasing interest in a range of issues, including stewardship of public funds, delivery of programs, accessibility to underrepresented populations, and faculty roles and responsibilities, as well as student access and mobility. It will be difficult (if not impossible) to change this situation. Although institutions might welcome less interest from policymakers—and may question the activism of policymakers and statewide boards—students in most states have benefited from policies that make it easier for them to attend college in the way they choose. Policy changes that increase the potential for student mobility have generally resulted from state policymakers' actions, not from institutional leadership. As representatives of the citizenry, over the past couple of decades lawmakers have been more responsive than many institutions to student concerns about transferability of credit, course delivery, and admissions.

The generally strong national and state economies in recent decades also have affected attendance patterns. Unemployment rates in the United States fell from 7.3 percent in 1991 to 4.0 percent in 2000, then surged upward again in 2001 to 5.8 percent (Bureau of Labor Statistics, 2002a, 2002b). A flush economy during the 1990s encouraged people to work but not necessarily increase their skills at the same time, resulting in a somewhat smaller market for part-time adult students. The number of part-time students over age twenty-five in degree-granting institutions was approximately 4.2 million in 1990; that number dropped to about 4.0 million by 1999 but is expected to rise to 4.6 million by 2010 (U.S. Department of Education, 2002). It is too early to know how the economic recession that began in 2001 and the drop in public confidence resulting from the recent corporate accounting scandals will influence college attendance.

Attendance patterns also have been affected by the rise of new market-driven providers, mainly large for-profit institutions such as the University of Phoenix. Supported by federal and state financial aid policies that enable eligible students to secure loans and grants while attending a wider range of institutions than was possible before, these institutions are flexible and open to students' needs. As a subset of higher education in America, these alternative institutions welcome students as consumers of higher education who want a high return on their investment and good service tailored to their needs. They understand that students demand the same level of service from colleges that they receive at their banks, supermarkets, and retail stores. For-profit institutions are a growing concern for traditional providers: among degree-granting for-profit institutions that participated in Title IV federal financial aid programs, total fall enrollment grew from nearly 304,500 in 1996 to over 430,000 in 1999 (U.S. Department of Education, 2002).

After this brief context setting, we will now look at a range of public policies and how they influence student attendance.

Financing Policies and Their Effect on Attendance Patterns. Foremost among the different kinds of state policies that influence attendance is finance. The way states distribute the responsibility for paying for higher education is reflected in their public policies—and these policies in turn can shape student attendance patterns. The primary state funding policies address direct appropriations to support institutions, tuition, and financial aid.

The "shared responsibility" approach that has dominated public higher education financing in the United States for recent generations means that students and their families, along with the state and federal government, help bear the burden of the cost of a college education. The state's share comes primarily through direct appropriations to institutions. Overall, appropriations of state tax funds for the operating expenses of higher education increased 59 percent between fiscal year 1992 and fiscal year 2002, but the *rate* of increase declined in the most recent year: between FY01 and FY02, the increase was only 4.6 percent, compared with 6.7 percent between FY00 and FY01 (*Grapevine,* 2002). Although dollar amounts in most states grew, other trends in state appropriations show that most states have reduced higher education's share of their budgets (U.S. Bureau of the Census, 2001). Higher education's share of state general fund appropriations as a percentage of tax revenue has declined steadily—from 12 percent in 1992 to 10.6 percent in 2000 (National Conference of State Legislatures, 1992, 2001). The share of state tax revenue appropriated to higher education also has dropped, from 13.4 percent in fiscal year 1991 to 11.8 percent in fiscal year 2001 (National Conference of State Legislatures, 1992, 2001). Over this period of generally strong state economic growth, higher education's share of state revenues did not grow; however, enrollments nationally increased from 13.8 million in 1990 to nearly 14.8 million in 1999—and are projected to reach 17.5 million by 2010 (U.S. Department of Education, 2002).

This financing policy, characterized by a decreasing state share, means that more of the cost of education is passed to the student in the form of tuition and other charges. Much has been written in the past few years on the price—and the underlying cost—of education. It may well be that rising prices have not dissuaded students from attending or changed the way they attend, as witnessed by rising enrollments. We simply do not know enough about why potential students do not enroll or why students leave and do not finish their degrees. Past research indicates that financial constraints have been a leading cause of dropping out, at least for students of limited means. There is mounting evidence that states that have funneled a smaller share of appropriations to higher education also have increased the price of education for most students. As Jane Wellman observed, "Since 1975, current-dollar tuition and fees have gone up almost fivefold at public institutions, primarily due to reductions in state funding. When state appropriations have dropped—as in the early 1990s—tuition has spiked" (Wellman, 2002a, p. 28). Though the ease of obtaining student loans may have ameliorated this problem somewhat, it seems reasonable to conclude that reduced state investment in the cost of education has had, and will continue to have, a chilling effect on whether people go to college, where they go, and how they attend.

As noted, the state uses three financing tools: direct appropriations for institutional operating expenses, tuition policy, and student financial aid. Most states reward their institutions because they fund on an enrollment-driven model where more bodies—or full-time-equivalent (FTE) students—means more money. This would suggest that institutions would want to attract and retain as many students as possible for as long as possible. An institution that places a high priority on retaining students will look for ways to do that, resulting in high persistence and low dropout levels—in short, reduced student mobility. Persistence and graduation data suggest, however, that, in general, institutions have been only moderately success-ful in retaining students to graduation: only half of all students who began college in 1989–90 had earned some type of degree by 1994 (U.S. Department of Education, 2001). That another 13 percent were still enrolled indicates that institutions are finding ways to keep students, and that students are finding ways to stay.

Perhaps the state policy tool that can have the greatest influence on attendance patterns—and where, or if, students go to college—is the second one, tuition. Tuition-setting authority resides primarily with the state legislature, although in some states the individual institution or system can set tuition or has some flexibility in determining tuition within a range established by the legislature. Whereas higher education has been allocated a smaller share of the fiscal pie over the past decade, student prices in the form of tuition and fees have increased. Average tuition and fees at public four-year institutions went from $2,107 in 1991–92 to $3,754 in 2001–02, a 78 percent increase in current dollars; at two-year institutions the increase was from $1,171 to $1,738, an increase of 48 percent (College Board, 2001). As a policy tool, tuition levels can have a dramatic effect on student atten-dance patterns—resulting in students not attending college at all, going only part-time, or choosing an institution where the price is lower or more finan-cial aid is available.

Differentiated tuition is the rule in states with both two- and four-year institutions. States with community colleges charge lower tuition and fees in those institutions, thus encouraging residents to attend the two-year col-leges. California, Florida, Arizona, and Washington have seen great growth in the numbers of students attending their two-year colleges. Students enroll in these schools for many different reasons, but price is clearly an impor-tant one. Students have responded favorably to lower-priced, quality insti-tutions, particularly when barriers to attending upper-division institutions are also reduced through strong articulation and transfer agreements. In addition, higher tuition at four-year institutions discourages unemployed students and those from low-income families, whose attendance patterns are very responsive to price differentials. An abundance of research shows pervasive enrollment of underrepresented minority groups and low-income students in less-than-baccalaureate institutions.

Both states and students influence the third state policy tool: financial aid. States with a policy of providing significant financial aid, especially need-based aid in a "high-tuition" environment, *should* stand a better chance of attracting students to higher education because aid results in less of a financial burden on the student. However, as reported in *Measuring Up 2000,* only a few states (California, Colorado, and Illinois, for example) received high grades for both participation and affordability; many received a high grade on one indicator but a lower grade on the other (National Center for Public Policy and Higher Education, 2000). This suggests that attendance may be less tied to tuition levels and financial aid than one might think. Concomitantly, students who are able to find financial aid from a source other than the state or who are willing to take on loan debt will enroll in higher numbers. The availability of aid has a direct impact on attendance patterns for some students; it may draw students from one institution to another and may be the deciding factor in an individual's decision to go to college.

Several problems emerge from financing policies as they currently exist in the states. One is that state policies relate only to per FTE costs that follow traditional attendance patterns. In some types of institutions—particularly community colleges—per-student costs are generally higher than in other kinds of institutions because many of the services that are available for full-time students must also be provided for part-time students who predominate at two-year institutions. Institutions often cannot provide these services in the same manner—part-timers need evening and weekend service, for instance, both of which are more expensive. Per FTE funding fails to cover adequately adult and part-time students, who are often marginalized, and if distance learning is added to the equation for these students, per FTE funding must be spread even further—for institutions often receive no additional financial support for technologically mediated delivery modes.

A second problem is that our funding models are past-oriented rather than future-oriented—they consider prior enrollment trends and thus will not capture changing student attendance patterns effectively. As increasing numbers of students choose to attend college less than full-time, colleges and universities will be less interested in attracting and serving these students because they will be considered "unfunded" or "underfunded."

Finally, current funding policies reward institutions for enrollment but ignore student success. Thus, a significant problem—lack of completion—goes untreated. Present financing policies do not hold anyone accountable for ensuring that students with different attendance patterns are supported or succeed. Our policies are designed to protect the providers of education rather than to respond to the needs of consumers.

Other Policies That Influence Attendance. Financing policies are a powerful stimulus for institutional and student behavior. But other policies also exert great pressure on students and their attendance decisions. An important one—financial aid—was mentioned earlier and will be revisited in this section. Other policies that will be discussed here are admissions, residency, articulation and transfer, course and program delivery, and accelerated options.

In Chapter Six King presents compelling information about the relationships between borrowing, working, student attendance patterns, and persistence. Long-standing financial aid policies at the federal, state, and institutional levels also have shaped student attendance patterns. The requirement of twelve credit hours for full-time attendance and financial aid eligibility in many federal and state aid programs is a prime example of a public policy that influences student attendance behavior. The policy not only sets parameters that support traditional students but locks part-timers out of many financial aid programs. Few states provide financial aid for part-timers. Federal programs that allow part-time attendance generally require at least half-time enrollment. Work-study financial aid programs can help ameliorate the need to attend part-time, but they too require a student to take at least twelve credit hours to qualify. Portability issues also affect student attendance. Lack of portability in state financial aid programs, especially merit-based aid, often keeps students in state and restricts their mobility to out-of-state institutions. Federal aid programs that move across state lines foster mobility and support students who want to attend multiple institutions.

A second area of potential policy influence on student attendance patterns is college admissions. Admissions policies are usually set by an institution or a system that represents multiple institutions. In general, institutions whose mission is to build a student body around first-time, first-year freshmen will have admissions policies that allow very small percentages of new students to enter as transfers and discourage less-than-full-time attendance. In some instances, the faculty may shape or refine institutional admissions policies to attract the kinds of students they want, but the faculty still represent the wishes of the institution, not the student. Open-door colleges usually are pleased to admit almost anyone, but may restrict students to nondegree programs if they do not meet program requirements.

Residency is a third policy area. Many states have stringent policies that prohibit out-of-state students from establishing residency for tuition purposes as long as they are in the state to pursue higher education. Because of the large difference between tuition levels for resident and nonresident students, these kinds of policies will force some nonresidents to attend part-time or not at all. State policymakers and some educators defend higher nonresident tuition on the grounds that the state's citizens should not have to subsidize the cost of college for nonresidents. Furthermore, departments often require that their students establish "residency" by completing a specified number of credits in a limited time frame. Or a program can make admission contingent on a student demonstrating that he or she will graduate in a specified length of time—for instance, four years. These additional requirements change the way that some students attend and where they attend.

One policy area where many states have made good progress in fostering student mobility is articulation and transfer. In a few states—Arizona and Florida, for example—student articulation is supported by statewide policies. A statewide agreement that protects the student and guarantees transfer of credit is a strong public policy mechanism for students. Mobility and attendance patterns will expand to the extent that students are not penalized (through credit loss or repetition of course work) for moving from one institution to another. A recent paper by Jane Wellman for the National Center for Public Policy and Higher Education examines the relationship between state postsecondary policy and the effectiveness of the community college–baccalaureate transfer function. She concludes that state policy can influence the effectiveness of statewide two-to-four transfer performance. "States that have a comprehensive, integrated approach to transfer policy seem to do better than those that focus primarily on transfer as an academic and institutional matter"(Wellman, 2002b, p. 16). Wellman also notes that no state is using all of the tools available to stimulate transfer performance, pointing out that student aid policy, goal setting, and rewarding transfer performance are some of those tools.

In most states, such a policy is represented in institution-to-institution rather than statewide agreements. In a few states, transfer is a smooth process that does not penalize students. In effect, statewide agreements have shifted student enrollment to community colleges and made it easier and more efficient for students to attend multiple institutions. Past problems with articulation and transfer, however, have resulted in a new phenomenon among community colleges: the push to offer baccalaureate degrees. This is playing out differently across two-year colleges and states, but student mobility may be impeded depending on the degree to which state policymakers allow two-year institutions to offer four-year degrees. Once again, state policy that supports articulated baccalaureate degrees among different kinds of institutions will encourage mobility and improve attendance. Policies that permit community colleges to provide the four-year degree will reduce mobility, but by responding to student needs, should improve attendance.

How students get their college education has been dramatically influenced by technologically mediated instruction. In some cases, this means that courses and full programs are delivered via technology; in others, portions of an individual course incorporate some form of technology. We have avoided here the term *distance education* because distance is often not the issue; on-campus students account for high percentages of on-line enrollment at their home institutions.

The opportunity to enroll in courses offered on-line through a vast array of quality postsecondary institutions and other providers has had an incredible impact on student attendance patterns. In Chapter Two, McCormick explored multi-institution attendance; on-line courses account for some of this multi-institutional work. Policies that support this behavior are now found primarily at the institutional and program level, but increasing numbers of states are looking at policies that address cost, quality, and other issues related to technology-mediated instruction. The growth in the number of states with policies that establish and provide for virtual universities is another indicator of how this delivery system will continue to increase opportunities for different attendance patterns. In addition, improvements in services, program quality, portability of credits, and financial aid all increase the attractiveness of this option. Institutional, if not state, policies that control these areas also increase the likelihood that students will take advantage of them.

Accelerated options—enrollment of high school students in college-level courses through dual and concurrent enrollment, advanced placement, and international baccalaureate programs—are other indicators of changing student attendance. Although data are not widely available on these programs, except for advanced placement, anecdotal information suggests that growing numbers of students are choosing these options. For example, the number of advanced placement candidates in 1990–91 was just under 360,000; that number grew to approximately 845,000 in 2000–01. Furthermore, the number of public schools nationally participating in the AP program increased from 9,786 to 13,680 during the same period (College Board, 2002). Policies increasingly support accelerated-learning opportunities and allow students to enter higher education with college credit awarded for successful completion of accelerated courses.

States vary in how they have managed accelerated options. By 2000, at least twenty-three states had established dual enrollment programs through legislation, while fifteen were operating through locally developed agreements involving a college and nearby school district (Frazier, 2000). Another option is seen in New Mexico's policy approach, which has been to develop a comprehensive, aligned "Framework for Accelerated Learning." This framework is the result of a joint effort between the Commission on Higher Education and the State Board of Education to develop a statewide policy for implementing strategies through a systematic approach to accelerated learning.

Each of the policy areas discussed in the preceding paragraphs has its problems. Some of the more immediate concerns relate to financial aid, because aid policies do not usually support attendance patterns that are not traditional or students that are not traditional. As noted, even aid programs like work-study, which could help students move from part-time to full-time attendance, are designed for traditional students. Broader eligibility requirements and higher wages for this program would assist students who are part-time but prefer to be full-time to make that change. Absent this support, we may be forcing students to work off campus and compromising their chances for completion.

Another concern is the lack of consistency among the states and by the federal government on whether students who take most of their courses online can qualify for financial aid. There are signs of change. At the national level there is consideration of revising federal aid policy that currently largely denies eligibility for aid to students participating in distance-education programs. From the students' perspective, it would seem that greater flexibility in aid for on-line courses would be a positive move. It would also seem that greater mobility and multi-institutional attendance would be a by-product of that flexibility. For institutions and systems with high enrollments in on-line courses, this may also be a positive change, but one that must be weighed against the potential loss in credit hours from traditional classroom courses and concern about the quality of courses.

In sum, there are abundant examples of how current federal, state, and institutional policies can foster or hinder student attendance. In the next section, we explore the public's willingness to sustain or expand support for diverse attendance patterns.

Capacity and Will of Public Policy to Address Attendance Issues

This chapter has so far focused on the question of how well past and present public policy addresses the needs of changing student attendance patterns. The answer has been "It depends"—on whether the students involved are young, financially able, and academically prepared, and whether the intentional efforts already in place have worked. This section of the chapter looks forward and examines whether public policy will have the capacity and will to address the changing needs of new students in the future using the four public policy approaches discussed earlier.

Financing Higher Education for the Public Good. The first question we must ask is whether public policy will provide sufficient support to sustain higher education as a public good. Unfortunately, there is little reason for optimism about future support of public higher education in responding to the needs of new students. This is true at both the state and federal levels. Both will simply lack the financial resources to sustain broad access to high-quality public postsecondary education, at least in the near future.

The 1999 report from the National Center for Public Policy and Higher Education entitled *State Spending for Higher Education in the Next Decade* documents structural budget deficits for most states (Hovey, 1999). Compounding this, as discussed earlier, the share of resources going to higher education in most states has declined and will likely continue to do so. The consequences will be much more dire for higher education in the next few years than in the recent past. In the past, higher education's smaller share of state resources was drawn from an overall pool of funds that was steadily rising, yielding increased funds for our colleges and universities. In the future, higher education's share will be taken from a static or declining pool of funds. Many states simply will not have the capacity to support higher education at past levels.

Demographic trends will exacerbate the dilemma for many states. Indeed, demographics present a double-edged sword. States that are growing rapidly—as are most in the West, Southwest, and Southeast—may not be able to boost funding sufficiently to support the higher level of services needed to satisfy demand. Conversely, states that are not growing will miss out on the marginal increase in revenue that growth provides to keep supply and demand balanced.

Similarly, it appears that the federal government will find it increasingly difficult to sustain a strong commitment to higher education, let alone enhance this commitment in response to the unique needs of students with changing attendance patterns. The massive tax cut adopted in fall 2001 will eliminate virtually any opportunity for increased discretionary federal spending; it may even require substantial cuts in such funding as the full impact of "tax relief" is felt over the next ten years (that is, unless we are willing to live with a new era of federal budget deficits). The impact of the tragic events of September 11, 2001, will further compound this difficulty, because costs related to homeland security will take a larger share of limited federal resources. We have already begun to witness this scenario unfolding with the federal Pell grant program; the maximum grant increased rapidly over the past eight years, from $2,300 to $4,000, but it is likely that growth will be difficult to sustain.

As we have seen, during an era of relatively substantial resources, we failed to provide the necessary support, both financial and academic, to ensure student success in the context of changing attendance patterns. Is it realistic, therefore, to expect that public policy will support these students adequately in the future when resources will not be as plentiful?

There are also mixed messages about whether the public will remains to sustain an ethic of inclusiveness. From 1958 to 1980, there was a sense that most if not all citizens could and should benefit from more education. Furthermore, the concept of *lifelong learning* became commonplace. That public consensus would appear to persist today: virtually every politician "believes" in lifelong learning and in ensuring broad access to higher education. Continuing fervor for this ethic clearly helped fuel Zell Miller's popularity in Georgia, where he introduced the now-famous HOPE scholarship program. And without doubt it also helped former President Bill Clinton, whose 1996 reelection bid was strengthened by his HOPE tax credits and lifelong learning deductions, both intended to make it possible for every American to get a higher education.

Signs of waning support for this ethic, however, have begun to appear. For example, although there is a measure of anxiety in some states over low "grades" on the *Measuring Up 2000* national report card, there is no great angst (National Center for Public Policy and Higher Education, 2000). If the past is prologue, some states will protect their investment in higher education despite the tough financial times ahead. But most see higher education as a discretionary expense, albeit a valuable one, that will be subject to reduction when cuts become imperative. Some policymakers have begun to wonder aloud if higher education really is appropriate for everyone, particularly these potential new students who are beginning to tax the capacity of our higher education system. We are beginning to hear these voices in public policy. For example, many states have become enamored of attracting the best and the brightest students, rewarding them through new merit-based student aid programs and special academic programs. Yet we see little of that same excitement for helping the neediest students through either traditional need-based financial aid programs or remedial-developmental programs that aim to ensure success for the academically underprepared.

In contrast, federal support has been quite substantial in the last few years. The amount of the Pell grant has increased by two-thirds over the past decade, twice the rate of inflation. Although federal funding will be harder to come by in the future (and though the ground lost in the 1980s has yet to be completely recovered), recent trends are promising. Yet these promising trends have done little to enhance support for students with changing attendance patterns. The federal government has been willing only to experiment with aiding students who receive their education primarily at a distance, even though such programs are clearly here to stay. States have been reluctant to revise funding policies to address the needs of new and different students. And both federal and state governments have failed to respond to the needs of "swirling" students, who receive their education at multiple institutions, even though this practice has become commonplace. Our policies still assume that these are the institutions' students, rather than the students' education.

We face another dilemma in this country, too: the way we manage and govern higher education is not well-suited to serving the needs of the twenty-first century, and particularly, the needs of new students with untraditional attendance patterns. Too often our policies, which have evolved piecemeal over time, do not fit together—the sum of the parts does not equal the intended whole. Public policy that supports institutions generally focuses on the delivery of quality services but seldom reinforces institutional behavior that enhances access or promotes the successful participation of marginal student populations. Furthermore, institutional finance strategies seldom intentionally integrate with tuition policy, which is generally seen only as a revenue generator and not as an integral component of higher education policy. And too often, neither institutional funding policy nor tuition policy intentionally interfaces with financial aid, which is generally perceived as a Band-Aid approach to affordability. Unless these funding policies— institutional support, tuition, and financial aid—are brought together, our financial management strategies will continue to be disjointed, antiquated, and an impediment to ensuring that all students who want and need a quality education can receive one.

One clue to whether public policy responds to these three dilemmas will be found in the direction in which resources flow as times get tough: to students who need them or to students who do not, to institutions that serve new students or to those that do not, or to services other than higher education.

Institutions will respond as large organizations respond to changing circumstances: in economically rational ways. First and foremost, they will strive to preserve the quality of the educational enterprise. In American higher education, quality is defined more by whom and how you serve than by what students learn, so institutions will certainly focus on which students they serve and how they serve them. To enhance perceived quality, institutions will become more selective, a practice that will work to the disadvantage of new student populations; these students come disproportionately from less educationally advantaged backgrounds. To enhance the educational process, institutions will focus on retaining and attracting the best faculty, many of whom will be more interested in doing research than in teaching, particularly if they must teach poorly prepared students. Again, this rational institutional reaction to tough times will mitigate against the new students. To support these interests, institutions will pursue new avenues of revenue, such as private industry support and higher tuition, which will also lead to less focus on traditional instruction and greater focus on new activities, such as customized instruction and research, serving full-pay students.

All this does not bode well for the new students with new attendance patterns. As usual, students with financial resources and strong academic backgrounds will not be at risk, whether they are young or old. But those with few resources and limited academic preparation easily could see access erode. Institutions facing severe financial constraints but exceptional demand (whether they are selective or not) will have little incentive to reach out to underserved populations; they will not need to in order to fill available seats and they will not be able to afford to do so. Witness the experience of the California State University system in the mid-1990s. The state of California was broke, so it reduced funding for higher education. As a result, its public institutions increased tuition and reduced access. That is not the way officials in California saw their actions, however: leaders in the CSU system claimed they were acting magnanimously by actually increasing enrollments, which indeed they did. But enrollment did not grow as rapidly as demand; the increase in enrollment actually represented a decline in the percentage of the population being served. Access eroded despite what public officials said and came to believe.

Contracting for Services. One way out of the financial crunch is to find less expensive methods to secure necessary services, and one approach gaining popularity in modern public policy is to contract for services. In truth, contracting for service is not new. The Western Commission for Higher Education (WICHE), for which the authors of this chapter work, has been brokering service contracts between states for fifty years. Through WICHE programs and those of other interstate regional compacts, states can ensure educational opportunity for their residents in fields of study that individual states cannot afford to sustain on their own. Contracting for service has also become standard operating procedure for addressing federal policy concerns. The federal government contracts with institutions to maintain foreign area studies departments, ensuring that the federal government has access to a repository of knowledge about all areas of the world. It contracts through the TRIO programs for services for at-risk middle school, high school, and college students. It contracts with banks and states to ensure the flow of federal loans to students and provides grants that for all practical purposes buy access into postsecondary education for many of the recipients.

As this bevy of activities suggests, contracts can be devised to serve new students with changing attendance patterns, and serve them well. Yet often contractors do not enter into such agreements because they understandably prefer to serve students who are *easy to serve*. It is cheaper to do so and easier to achieve performance expectations. Even our WICHE programs, which work well with traditional students, do not serve as well new students with changing attendance patterns.

Contracting has attracted attention in the current political environment because it appeals to our current infatuation with privatization. Increasingly, public policy is based on policymakers' faith in market forces to govern both private and public policy. Nevertheless, the actual resources committed to such activities are modest compared with the subsidies traditionally provided to public institutions.

Incentive Funding. In the third approach to public policy noted at the beginning of this chapter, government acts as a catalyst to encourage others to pursue activities consistent with the public agenda. This concept of providing incentives for others to do the right thing has become an increasingly popular approach. An excellent example of this policy at the federal level is the Fund for the Improvement of Postsecondary Education (FIPSE). For twenty-five years, a modest federal financial commitment to FIPSE has helped spawn some of the most innovative and valuable ideas to improve the management and delivery of quality higher education in America. Recently, the 1998 reauthorization of the Higher Education Act created the Learning Anytime Anyplace Partnership (LAAP) program to provide an incentive for institutions of higher education, in collaboration with private-sector entrepreneurs, to find new ways to serve students effectively through technology-mediated instruction. The GEAR UP program, created in the same legislation, provides the catalyst for institutions to partner with middle schools, high schools, community groups, and others to help at-risk youth better prepare for continuing their education beyond high school. Obviously, this incentive can and has been used as a vehicle for supporting the needs of new students with changing attendance patterns.

This approach, however, generally works only if there is strong support from the higher education community (as was the case with creation of the GEAR UP program) or if the federal interest is compelling and reasonably novel (as was the case for the LAAP program). At this time, there is little reason to believe that either of these conditions will drive public policy focused on serving the changing nature of new students.

Governmental Laws and Regulations. Two of the most significant areas in which the government has mandated actions by others to lead to the desired public outcome are regulation and accountability.

The Value of Regulation. Without a doubt, regulation today is out of vogue. The U.S. Department of Education, through negotiated rule making, and the Congress, through its FED UP regulatory reform initiative, are working hard to one-up each other on who can claim greater dedication to deregulation. Yet, regulation continues to thrive. How can this be? It is because we need and secretly recognize the value of regulation, even if such rules are unpopular.

Regulations usually are prompted by one of two circumstances: market forces have failed to respond to a public concern ("market failure") or the risk to the public is simply too high to wait and see if the market will succeed or fail. The actions of the U.S. Department of Education in the early 1990s to tighten regulations on for-profit proprietary schools because of their high default rates are a good example of regulatory response to market failure. The current flurry of regulatory actions around homeland security—from new procedures in airports to restrictions on international students studying in this country—are examples of regulations created in the face of perceived high risk.

The future regulatory picture is murky. Although current rhetoric at both the federal and state levels appears to favor the relaxation of regulations on educational providers to ensure broader access to new students, at least in the case of traditional education provided to traditional students, the future of regulation when it comes to new students and new providers is less clear. There continues to be much discussion about relaxing the regulation of new providers, particularly those offering education through new technologies, but little actual change has occurred. Furthermore, there seems to be little interest in relaxing regulations as they apply to nontraditional students, particularly those without financial resources. In part this is because some Washington, D.C.–based groups are concerned that students, and particularly educationally disadvantaged students, will not be well served by deregulation. These groups fear that, absent good regulation, many institutions will return to the policies and practices of the 1980s— using, abusing, and abandoning students and capturing their financial assistance but not educating them well in exchange.

Accountability as a Public Policy Tool. Accountability measures have increasingly become a subtle and effective tool for advancing public policy as policy analysis and public administration have matured as professions in public service. There is no reason to believe that this focus on accountability will subside.

Accountability may, in fact, hold great promise for addressing issues of new students and changing attendance patterns. The first step in creating good accountability systems is strong, credible information and analysis. As databases improve and better information results, we will have a more complete picture of how current patterns of attendance affect student success. In Chapter Six of this volume, for example, King uses good information and policy analysis to examine factors of attendance that contribute to or detract from success for students who pursue new attendance patterns. Such policy analyses will help institutions and governments to discern how current policies and practices affect today's changing students, how they must change, and how students should be encouraged to change to achieve greater success. As the demand for public accountability in higher education has grown in recent years, it has become increasingly apparent that some accountability schemes are more effective in addressing real public policy issues than others. Some accountability measures accurately capture performance, whereas others truly miss the point. And experience has shown that good policy analysis, based on solid data, is key to providing informed and legitimate accountability measures.

Furthermore, accountability measures also can be used to prod those institutions and governments that are reticent to change. Information is a powerful tool that can help improve the efficacy of each of the other public policy approaches previously discussed. For example, *Measuring Up 2000,* the report from the National Center for Public Policy and Higher Education (2000), has influenced public policy discussions in two very important ways. First, it has added a new dimension of data to help states understand where they stand compared with others. Second, the gaps and limitations of the data in this report have helped prompt support for better databases to strengthen future accountability measures.

Another reason why accountability is particularly well-suited to today's public policy arena is that it is the logical trade-off for the greater autonomy that so many public higher education leaders are currently requesting. In a number of states—Hawaii, Oregon, and North Dakota, to name a few—greater accountability has been the explicit quid pro quo for receiving greater autonomy in the administration of public institutions of higher education.

Yet public accountability remains suspect and uncomfortable for many in higher education. In part, that is because we all say we believe in accountability, but truth be known, would rather be left alone. In part, it is because accountability, as it has evolved, has not always been fair or effective. Policymakers too often have measured the wrong things, focusing too heavily on inputs into the educational process or educational process factors themselves rather than on socially desirable educational outcomes, such as whether students learn what they need to learn and whether these learning outcomes are equitably distributed among all students. As accountability evolves, however, it will improve, and it will remain an essential and increasingly prevalent public policy tool.

Conclusion

It appears that, at least in the near future, public policy likely will be more reactive than proactive and more iterative than creative in responding to the needs and concerns of students with new attendance patterns. Swirling students will likely swirl even more among institutions, but it will take some time for our policies to catch up to the idea that *they* get to choose the education they want and that *we* do not choose for them. Economically disadvantaged students will continue to face substantial financial hardship, probably more in the future than today, as tuitions increase without requisite increases in need-based aid, and as states, facing substantial budget shortfalls, pass the buck in higher education to the consumer.

Despite this pessimism, there are certainly some bright signs. The recent emergence of important new early intervention efforts, such as the Pathways to College and GEAR UP programs, will better prepare more educationally disadvantaged students for college. We also hear much more public policy concern expressed about student persistence and completion. Nevertheless, little has changed in funding strategies, which continue to reward institutions for serving the most academically and financially advantaged students. Too little public policy focuses on restructuring the culture of our educational institutions in ways that will support greater student success—and there is little reason to believe this will change.

There are certainly ways for public policy to support greater success for new students taking new paths—for example, broader use of cooperative work-study programs, greater focus on supporting successful remedial and developmental instruction, and more support for faculty whose students learn and stay. But there is little evidence that these strategies will win the day in an era of limited resources, and apparently, waning public will for widening participation. Ironically, America seems to be moving away from this ideal just as the rest of the world is poised to adopt it and invest more in education. Others have learned the value of broad educational access to economic and social vitality, and many have learned it from the United States. Yet in America we have begun to take it for granted, and we seem less willing to sacrifice to secure this benefit, at least as a public good. Go figure.

References

Bok, D. *Higher Learning*. Cambridge, Mass.: Harvard University Press, 1986.
Bureau of Labor Statistics. *Local Area Unemployment Statistics*. [http://data.bls.gov/lab-java/outside.jsp?survey=la]. 2002a.

Bureau of Labor Statistics. "Labor Force Statistics." *Current Population Survey.* [http://data.bls.gov/servlet/SurveyOutputServlet?series_id=LFS21000000]. 2002b.

College Board. *Trends in College Pricing.* New York: College Board, 2001.

College Board. *Participation in AP: Annual Participation.* New York: College Board. [http://apcentral.collegeboard.com/program/participation/0,1289,150–156–0–0,00.html]. 2002.

Frazier, C. M. *Dual Enrollment: A Fifty-State Overview.* Dual Credit Study Technical Report no. 2. Seattle: Institute for Educational Inquiry, Oct. 2000.

Grapevine: A National Database of Tax Support for Higher Education. [http://www.coe.ilstu.edu/grapevine/50state.htm]. 2002.

Hovey, H. A. *State Spending for Higher Education in the Next Decade.* San Jose, Calif.: National Center for Public Policy and Higher Education, 1999.

National Center for Public Policy and Higher Education. *Measuring Up 2000.* San Jose, Calif.: National Center for Public Policy and Higher Education, 2000.

National Conference of State Legislatures. *State Budget Actions: 1992.* Denver, Colo.: National Conference of State Legislators, 1992.

National Conference of State Legislatures. *State Budget Actions: 2000.* Denver, Colo.: National Conference of State Legislators, 2001.

U.S. Bureau of the Census. *State Government Tax Collections.* Washington, D.C.: U.S. Bureau of the Census, 2001.

U.S. Department of Education, National Center for Education Statistics. *The Condition of Education 2001* (NCES 2001–072). Washington, D.C.: U.S. Government Printing Office, 2001.

U.S. Department of Education, National Center for Education Statistics. *Digest of Education Statistics 2001* (NCES 2002–130). Washington, D.C.: U.S. Government Printing Office, 2002.

Wellman, J. V. *Weathering the Double Whammy.* Washington, D.C.: Association of Governing Boards of Universities and Colleges, 2002a.

Wellman, J. V. *State Policy and Community College/Baccalaureate Transfer.* San Jose, Calif.: National Center for Public Policy and Higher Education, 2002b.

DAVID A. LONGANECKER *is executive director at the Western Interstate Commission for Higher Education.*

CHERYL D. BLANCO *is senior program director at the Western Interstate Commission for Higher Education.*

Working more than part-time and attending college part-time negatively affect persistence, especially among low-income students. Such choices also impede the ability of institutions to shorten time-to-degree, improve graduation rates, and accommodate larger numbers of students. Judicious use of student loans can help students reduce hours at work and finance full-time attendance.

Nontraditional Attendance and Persistence: The Cost of Students' Choices

Jacqueline E. King

Every day, students make decisions that affect their ability to complete a degree. They weigh some of these choices carefully, such as which college to attend. Yet they underestimate the impact of many other choices, such as whether to drop a course or accept more hours at work, not understanding the cumulative effect these decisions might have on their likelihood of completing a degree. Having more information on the consequences of student choices may help institutions design counseling interventions and other programs that can influence students to make decisions that improve their chances of persistence. Given that more than half of all undergraduates attend college part-time and 80 percent work while enrolled (U.S. Department of Education, 2002), it is crucial that institutions understand and confront the effects of student choices on academic success.

This chapter examines the most recent evidence on the effects of students' choices—all of which are financial to some extent—on their prospects of succeeding in college. It pays particular attention to the financing choices of low-income students, because these are at greatest risk of dropping out. The chapter addresses two main questions: How do students pay for college, and how do the financing patterns of low-income students differ from those of other students? What is the impact of students' financing choices on their academic success?

Note: This chapter is based on *Crucial Choices: How Students' Financial Decisions Affect Their Academic Success* (King, 2002).

Why should these questions matter to campus leaders? They matter because colleges increasingly will be challenged to maintain and enhance graduation rates, and in many cases, to shorten time-to-degree. As the student population becomes more diverse in age, race-ethnicity, and socio-economic status, it will become more difficult to improve graduation rates. Understanding the critical links between students' financial decisions and academic success—especially among low-income students—will help campuses continue to refine their efforts to help all students succeed.

Data and Limitations

The data for this chapter come from two national studies conducted by the U.S. Department of Education's National Center for Education Statistics. The *National Postsecondary Student Aid Study: 1995–96* (NPSAS) (U.S. Department of Education, 1996) provides a comprehensive national picture of how students pay for college in a single year. It includes data from college records, student interviews, and federal student financial aid files for more than thirty-five hundred undergraduate and graduate students. First-time freshmen made up a subset of the students studied in the 1995–96 iteration of NPSAS; this group was questioned again in fall 1998. The resulting longitudinal data set is called *Beginning Postsecondary Students Longitudinal Study: 1995–1998* (BPS) (U.S. Department of Education, 1998). This chapter will rely on the BPS data to examine persistence among students who began college in 1995–96. Although the three-year window does not allow researchers to study bachelor's degree completion, it does measure the percentage of students who have persisted into their junior year and are well on their way to completing their degree. All analysis in this chapter is by the author.

This chapter will examine only undergraduates, because the BPS study encompasses only undergraduate students and no comparable national data exist for graduate students. Furthermore, the financial resources and types of financial aid available to graduate and undergraduate students differ so sharply, and there are so many important distinctions among different types of graduate students, that it would be impossible to describe both graduate and undergraduate students adequately in a single publication. Because most policy discussions center on undergraduates, those students will be the subject of this chapter.

Definition of Low-Income Students

Determining who is a low-income student might seem, at first, to be a simple matter, but this is not the case. Several characteristics should be considered to make a fair determination of which college students truly fit the definition. The characteristics considered in this chapter are *dependency status, attendance status,* and *family size.*

The first step in assessing family income is to divide undergraduates into three groups: dependent students, independent students without dependents, and independent students with dependents. Dependent students are under age twenty-five, unmarried, not veterans, and without children. When dependent students apply for financial aid, their parents' income and assets are considered in the determination of their financial need. Students are considered independent—and count only their own income and that of a spouse when applying for aid—if they are twenty-five or older, married, a veteran, or have children. Independent students are further divided into those who do and do not have dependents. These distinctions are critical when assessing student income.

The second consideration is attendance status. This characteristic is particularly important when assessing independent students' income. Some independent students may seem quite poor, but if they are attending college full-time, this "poverty" may be a temporary condition. To control for this problem, this chapter uses students' income from the year prior to entering college.

Family size is the third characteristic used to determine which students are low-income. A family of four with an income of $30,000 usually is worse off than a family of two with the same income. The analysis in this chapter takes family size into account by converting income to a percentage of the federal poverty standard, which varies by family size. Because the federal poverty thresholds are very low, this chapter considers students low-income if their income equals 150 percent of the poverty threshold or less. Eight out of ten entering students falling into this income category who attended college at least half-time and applied for aid received a Pell grant, the primary federal grant for low-income students. Throughout the chapter, low-income students are compared with middle- and upper-income students, who had incomes of at least 300 percent of the poverty level.

Thirty-two percent of undergraduates who began college in 1995–96 came from families with incomes equal to or less than 150 percent of the poverty threshold, and 41 percent came from families with incomes equal to at least 300 percent of the poverty threshold. When dependency status is considered along with income, 65 percent of beginning students fall into one of three groups: low-income dependent students (17 percent of all beginning students), low-income independent students with dependents (11 percent), and middle- and upper-income dependent students (37 percent). The average income of students in these three groups ranged from $8,900 for low-income independent students with dependents to approximately $82,000 for middle- and upper-income dependent students.

Students' Financing Decisions

Students draw on many different resources to pay for college. Most begin with a certain amount of family resources—primarily in the form of income—and they choose institutions that vary in how much they charge and how much grant aid they have available. Students also make choices that determine their living expenses, such as whether to live on campus or at home. Then they make up whatever difference exists between their total student budget (adjusted for their attendance pattern and living situation, and reduced by any grant aid they may have received) and their family's resources through a combination of work, loans, and, increasingly, credit cards. The BPS data describe the different means and financing choices of low-income students and their more affluent peers.

Institutional Type and Price. Whether for academic or financial reasons (or a combination of the two), low-income students are more likely than their more affluent peers to choose institutions that offer programs of two years or less. Low-income students are somewhat more likely than their middle- and upper-income peers to attend public community and vocational colleges (50 percent versus 42 percent) and are far more likely to attend two-year and less-than-two-year for-profit institutions (21 percent versus 4 percent). Conversely, low-income students are less likely than middle- and upper-income students to attend public and private not-for-profit four-year institutions. More than half of middle- and upper-income freshmen in 1995–96 began at four-year institutions, compared with 30 percent of low-income freshmen.

The total student budget includes institutional charges for tuition, fees, and on-campus room and board for a full-time, full-year student, as well as institutions' estimates of expenses for items such as books and supplies, transportation, and entertainment. (The estimates shown here reflect institutions' best approximation of the amount students reasonably should spend on these items but cannot reflect the wide variance in student choices.) Low-income students save money by choosing institutions with shorter academic programs, not lower prices. Overall, low-income students in 1995–96 chose institutions with an average annual total student budget that was about $1,500 less than the average price of institutions chosen by middle- and upper-income students. Thus, low-income students are somewhat more likely to attend low-priced community colleges and are less likely to attend more expensive four-year institutions. However, 21 percent of low-income students chose for-profit institutions, which carried an average annual total student budget of $10,000. Low-income students face annual prices that are similar to those paid by their middle- and upper-income peers, but because they are more likely to attend two-year and less-than-two-year institutions, their total multiyear educational costs are less.

When low-income students choose among institutions of the same type, they generally do not make choices that save them much money. For example, when choosing among public four-year colleges, low-income undergraduates selected institutions with an average total student budget price $1,000 lower than the average total budget of institutions chosen by middle- and upper-income freshmen. At private four-year institutions, price seemed to be a slightly more important factor: the average total budget for low-income students attending private institutions was lower than the average total budget for middle- and upper-income students by about $4,300.

At community colleges and for-profit institutions, there was little difference in the average price of institutions chosen by low-income students and their middle- and upper-income peers.

The finding that low-income students do not tend to choose less expensive institutions is not as surprising as it initially may appear. Price is only one factor among many that students consider when choosing an institution. Location, selectivity, and curricular offerings all play a big role in student choice. In fact, when asked to name the most important factor influencing their choice of institution, low-income students were no more likely to name price than middle- and upper-income students.

Attendance Status, Living Arrangement, and Adjusted Student Budget. Other factors influencing the prices that students pay are attendance status (whether they attend on a full-time or part-time basis and for either a full or partial academic year) and living situation (whether they live on the campus, off campus, or with their parents). The overall beginning student population is split almost evenly between those who study full-time, full year (53 percent) and those who attend part-time or part year (47 percent). Low-income beginning students are less likely to study full-time, full year than middle- and upper-income freshmen (42 percent versus 64 percent). Of course, the prevalence of less-than-full-time and full-year attendance varies by type of institution. For example, one-quarter of entering students at for-profit institutions attend full-time, full year, versus nearly 80 percent of entering students at private four-year institutions. (It should be noted that, in this analysis, a full academic year is considered nine months. Many for-profit institution programs are shorter; students attending such programs full-time would not be considered full-time, full year in this analysis.) At all types of institutions, low-income students are less likely than middle- and upper-income students to attend full-time, full year.

In terms of living arrangements, 30 percent of all beginning students live on campus, 27 percent live off campus, and 43 percent live with their parents or other relatives. Most two-year and less-than-two-year institutions do not offer on-campus student housing. At four-year institutions, almost two-thirds of beginning students live on campus. Low-income students are far less likely than middle- and upper-income students to live on campus at four-year institutions (45 percent versus 75 percent). Part of the explanation is that many low-income students are older and have their own families; these students may prefer to remain in their existing homes or apartments, or the institution they attend may not offer suitable accommodations. Another explanation is that low-income students are twice as likely as middle- and upper-income students to live with their parents. At four-year institutions, 35 percent of low-income freshmen live with their parents, compared with 16 percent of middle- and upper-income beginners. There are many reasons why students might choose this option, but the cost savings is likely the primary one.

When the total student budget is adjusted for students' attendance status and housing choices, the average price for all entering undergraduates drops by 20 percent. At community colleges and for-profit institutions, where most students study part-time and many live at home, the average adjusted student budget is lower than the average total student budget by $2,600 and $3,000, respectively. This amount varies little by student income. At both public and private four-year institutions, where students are more likely to live on campus and study full-time, there is less difference between the average total and adjusted student budget. At public institutions, these choices reduce the average student budget only by some $1,000. Again, this amount varies little by income. Low-income students at private four-year institutions save more than their middle- and upper-income peers; their average adjusted student budget is approximately $2,200 less than the average total student budget. For middle- and upper-income students at these institutions, the average adjusted student budget is $1,250 less than the average total student budget. Of course, averages can mask great variation; some students reap significant savings by attending part-time or living at home. Nonetheless, in general, students make living and attendance choices that save relatively little money.

By contrast, students' attendance and housing choices can significantly affect their ability to succeed in college. Attending full-time may result in higher annual costs but it also can shorten time-to-degree, resulting in lower total expenses over a college career. In addition, research has consistently shown that students who attend college full-time are more likely to complete a degree than those who attend part-time; studies also have shown that students who live on campus are more likely to persist than students who live off campus or with their parents (Pascarella and Terenzini, 1991).

Grants and Net Price. Eighty-three percent of low-income freshmen applied for financial aid for the 1995–96 academic year. In contrast, 62 percent of all middle- and upper-income freshmen applied for assistance. Most students—and especially those with incomes less than 150 percent of the poverty threshold—will likely receive assistance if they apply for financial aid. Among low-income freshmen, 86 percent of those who applied for financial aid received grant assistance averaging $2,857. Approximately half of entering middle- and upper-income students who applied for aid received grants, but the average amount that these students received was slightly greater, at $3,322. This difference in average grant aid received reflects the fact that a higher proportion of middle- and upper-income students attend more expensive private institutions that offer significant amounts of institutional grant assistance.

When grant assistance is taken into account—in addition to living situation and attendance pattern—the average net price for all entering students (those who did and did not receive grants) is reduced by 33 percent, compared with the total student budget price. Grants reduce the average price for low-income students by 45 percent—or by $3,700 to $7,750—depending on type of institution. When grants are deducted, low-income students face substantially lower prices than middle- and upper-income students, especially at four-year institutions. This pattern reflects the fact that most grant assistance is awarded based on financial need, and low-income students, of course, demonstrate more need than students with greater financial resources. Despite this grant assistance, low-income students still must pay an average of $5,400. This is equivalent to 42 percent and 61 percent of average family income, respectively, for those who are dependent and for those who are independent with dependents. In contrast, the $8,745 average net price faced by middle- and upper-income dependent students is equivalent to only 11 percent of their average family income.

Student Loans. Despite the serious burden imposed by the price of college, low-income students are not much more likely to take out student loans than middle- and upper-income undergraduates. One-third of low-income freshmen received student loans in 1995–96, versus 27 percent of middle- and upper-income entering students. Because annual borrowing limits in the federal student loan programs are relatively low ($2,625 for dependent freshmen and $6,625 for independent freshmen), the amount borrowed by low-income students and that borrowed by middle- or upper-income students varies little. Among both groups, the average loan is about $3,000. Also among both income groups, relying on student loans is a less popular choice than either attending part-time or living at home.

Although many low-income students avoid student loans as freshmen, those low-income students who persist to a bachelor's degree are more likely to borrow and accrue more debt than their middle- and upper-income peers. Independent students, in particular, often accrue substantial debt because federal loan programs allow them to borrow more money annually than dependent students.

Unmet Need and Employment. When the expected family contribution (EFC), grants, loans, and other assistance (such as employer aid) are deducted from the adjusted institutional price, the remaining amount is a student's unmet need. (EFC is defined by a federal formula that takes into account student income, and in the case of dependents, parental income, assets, family size, and number of family members in college.) When students have no unmet need, it means that they have received enough aid to pay the entire net price of college, less the EFC. Low-income students face a lower average net price than middle- and upper-income students, but because low-income students have so few resources, their average unmet need is more than three times the average unmet need of middle- and upper-income undergraduates ($3,556 versus $994). Except at for-profit institutions, low-income freshmen have approximately $2,400 more average unmet need than middle- and upper-income freshmen. At for-profit institutions, low-income students face over $4,000 more in average unmet need than their middle- and upper-income peers.

To compensate for their unmet need, most students work during the academic year. Interestingly, despite their higher unmet need, low-income students are somewhat less likely to work than their middle- and upper-income peers: 63 percent of low-income freshmen worked during the 1995–96 academic year, compared with 71 percent of middle- and upper-income students. However, low-income dependent students are as likely to work, and to work about the same number of hours per week, as middle- and upper-income dependent students. Low-income independent students with dependents—who account for more than one-third of low-income freshmen—are less likely to work than their dependent peers, most likely because of their child-rearing responsibilities.

Furthermore, differences in income seem to have little impact on the role that work plays in a student's life. Students were asked whether they considered themselves primarily students who worked to meet college expenses or primarily employees who also attended classes. Only one-third of working low-income students and one-quarter of middle- and upper-income working students considered themselves employees who studied. But although they considered themselves students first, they worked an average of twenty-four hours per week.

In sum, low-income students generally do not choose institutions that are significantly less expensive than those chosen by middle- and upper-income students. Instead, their most common strategies for lowering their college expenses are, in order of frequency, applying for aid, working, and attending college part-time (see Figure 6.1). The least popular strategy for students at all income levels is taking out student loans.

Financing Choices and Persistence

These financing choices can have a substantial impact on students' academic success. Table 6.1 shows the percentage of 1995–96 first-time freshmen who had either attained a certificate or degree, were still enrolled, or had dropped out by fall 1998, for each of the financing choices detailed earlier. It shows that some 32 percent of all 1995–96 entering freshmen had dropped out with no degree by the spring of 1998, 19 percent still were enrolled at two-year or less-than-two-year institutions, 37 percent still were enrolled at four-year institutions, and 11 percent had earned an associate degree or certificate and left higher education. In general, students who were least likely to drop out pursued a very traditional pattern: they began at four-year institutions, studied full-time, lived on campus, and worked part-time—that is, one to fourteen hours per week. (It is important to note some students may have had no intention of completing a degree or certificate program; this is particularly likely at community colleges.)

This basic pattern varied somewhat by income. Middle- and upper-income students were less likely to have dropped out than low-income students. One-quarter of middle- and upper-income freshmen had left college

Figure 6.1. Financing Choices of Beginning Postsecondary Students, 1995–96

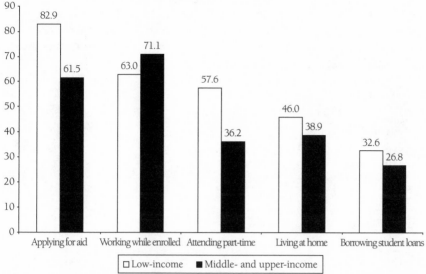

Source: U.S. Department of Education, National Center for Education Statistics, *Beginning Postsecondary Student Longitudinal Study: 1995–1998*, 1998.

without a degree by 1998, compared with 40 percent of low-income freshmen. For both groups of students, starting at a four-year institution, attending full-time, living on campus, and working part-time were associated with better-than-average persistence. Having a student loan and working part-time produced the lowest dropout rate for both groups of students, but middle- and upper-income students who did not work also persisted at high rates, regardless of whether they borrowed. Borrowing had a stronger effect on low-income students: those who borrowed and worked part-time performed better than those who worked part-time but did not borrow.

The importance of combining student loans with part-time work in the persistence of low-income students may be explained by the relationship between work and borrowing, on the one hand, and attendance status and institution type, on the other. Low-income students who borrowed and worked part-time were far more likely to attend on a full-time, full-year basis; 82 percent of these students attended full-time and for a full year. In contrast, only 27 percent of those who did not borrow and worked fifteen hours per week or more attended full-time, full year. Interestingly, low-income students who did not work at all were less likely to attend full-time than those who worked part-time. Of course, some low-income students—especially single parents—simply do not have the time to work or may jeopardize government benefits, such as food stamps, by working. Even among dependent students, those who worked part-time were more likely to attend

Table 6.1. 1995–1996 Beginning Postsecondary Students' Degree Attainment and Enrollment Status as of 1998 by First-Year Financing Choices

	No Degree, Not Enrolled (%)	Still Enrolled, Two-Year or Less (%)	Still Enrolled, Four-Year (%)	Attained an A.A. or Certificate (%)
All students	32.3	19.4	37.4	10.8
Institution type:				
Public two-year or less	43.6	32.6	14.4	9.4
Public four-year	18.8	6.3	72.7	1.7
Private four-year	17.2	5.3	75.7	1.5
For-profit two-year or less	34.8	11.4	2.7	51.2
Attendance pattern:				
Full-time, full year	15.8	14.9	60.5	8.6
Less than full-time, full year	48.0	23.3	15.6	13.0
Residence:				
On campus	15.4	5.7	76.5	2.1
Off campus	44.7	19.0	18.3	17.5
With parents or relatives	36.1	28.4	23.8	11.7
Filed financial aid application:				
No	37.3	25.0	29.0	8.5
Yes	30.5	17.3	40.5	11.5
Borrowed federal student loan:				
No	35.4	22.9	32.0	9.5
Yes	25.0	10.7	50.2	13.7
Hours worked per week while enrolled:				
None	26.7	14.9	44.1	14.2
1 to 14	15.8	13.2	64.8	5.7
15 to 34	30.6	26.7	31.7	10.8
35 or more	52.8	20.9	14.6	11.6
Working and borrowing status:				
Borrowed, did not work	25.5	8.5	50.4	15.4
Borrowed, worked 1 to 14 hours	10.6	6.0	78.3	4.4
Borrowed, worked 15+ hours	27.6	16.2	38.5	17.1
Did not borrow, did not work	27.3	18.2	40.9	13.6
Did not borrow, worked 1 to 15 hours	21.4	13.8	58.8	5.4
Did not borrow, worked 16+ hours	42.0	26.6	22.4	8.8

Note: Numbers may not add to 100 percent due to rounding.

Source: U.S. Department of Education, National Center for Education Statistics, Beginning Postsecondary Student Longitudinal Study: 1995–1998, 1998.

full-time, full year than those who did not work. Low-income students who combine borrowing with part-time work can best afford—both financially and in terms of time—to attend on a full-time, full-year basis. Those who forgo borrowing and work more than part-time may have every intention of attending full-time but drop to less than a full-time courseload because they cannot manage full-time attendance *and* a heavy work schedule.

Among low-income students, having a student loan and working one to fourteen hours per week also are highly correlated with attendance at a four-year institution—another important predictor of persistence. Three out of four students who borrowed and worked part-time attended a four-year institution, compared with just 18 percent of those who did not borrow and worked fifteen hours per week or more. Most likely, both work and borrowing were necessary for low-income students to afford a four-year institution. Nonetheless, students at two-year and less-than-two-year institutions who borrowed and worked part-time were far less likely to drop out than other students at these institutions. Only 9 percent of these students had dropped out by 1998, compared with 45 percent of all low-income students who began at two-year or less-than-two-year institutions. The pattern is similar, if not as dramatic, at four-year institutions. Some 13 percent of low-income students at four-year institutions who borrowed and worked part-time as freshmen had dropped out by 1998, compared with 27 percent of all low-income students at these institutions.

Thus, borrowing and working part-time are clearly associated with success for students at all income levels, especially for low-income students, yet less than 6 percent of freshmen adopted this strategy. In fact, the largest group of freshmen (44 percent) chose the financing strategy that is least associated with success: borrowing nothing and working fifteen or more hours per week. As discussed, this pattern varies little with student income. Even those students who could best afford to follow this strategy chose instead to avoid student loans and work fifteen or more hours per week.

Why are students making counterproductive choices? One explanation may be that students assume it will be less expensive in the long run to attend college part-time and avoid student loan debt. For many students, this is not the case. Of course, for those who drop out because they cannot adequately juggle college with work, the cost of working too many hours while enrolled is enormous. These individuals will pay for the rest of their lives in lost earning power. However, even those students who simply extend their undergraduate careers will pay in opportunity costs because they are delaying their entry into the job market as full-time, college-educated workers.

Exhibit 6.1 illustrates the costs of this approach for two students attending a public four-year institution. Wendy does not borrow, works twenty-five hours per week, and as a result, must take an extra year to graduate. Once her extra-educational expenses are deducted from her earnings, she nets $5,800 during her fifth year of college. (This analysis assumes that the living expenses of both students are the same, and as a result, excludes those costs.) Paul borrows $2,500 each year, allowing him to work only fourteen hours per week, and thus can graduate in four years. During the fifth year, Paul, now a graduate, earns $30,000. Even if the total cost of his $10,000 loan is assigned to that first year after graduation, Paul nets $15,756. In this scenario, working twenty-five hours per week cost Wendy about $10,000. Each student's situation will differ, and this simple simulation ignores many other costs that students may incur when they either stay

Exhibit 6.1. Income and Expenses Associated with Work and Borrowing: Two Scenarios

Wendy

Works 25 hours per week @ $7.50 per hour during academic year for 32 weeks	$6,000
Works 40 hours per week @ $7.50 per hour during breaks for 16 weeks	$4,800
Total income	$10,800
Fifth year of tuition, books, and supplies	$5,000
Total expenses	$5,000
Net gain	$5,800

Paul

Earnings from post-B.A. job	$30,000
Total income	$30,000
Borrowed $10,000 to compensate for working 15 hours per week over four academic years	
($7.50 per hour for 15 hours per week over 32 weeks = $3,600)	
$6,000 − $3,600 = $2,400	
$2,400 for four years = approx. $10,000)	
Total cost of $10,000 loan 7.5% interest over 10 years	$14,244
Total expenses	$14,244
Net gain	$15,756

Note: Living expenses are assumed to be constant in both scenarios.

in college or move into the workforce. For some students, working and taking a longer time to graduate may be unavoidable, and in some cases, might even be in their best financial interests. The problem is that students appear to be making these choices without considering the kinds of calculations Exhibit 6.1 illustrates.

A similar scenario might be developed to calculate the relative expense of attending college part-time or living off campus. It seems reasonable to assume—given the data presented here—that many students make crucial choices based on misinformation or faulty assumptions about the relative cost of the various options. These choices have serious consequences for all students, but they deal the hardest blow to low-income students—many of whom are first-generation college attendees who are not adequately prepared academically.

Student choices also have important consequences for institutions. Every institution wants—and is expected by key stakeholders—to have a high graduation rate. If a large proportion of the student body is working and attending part-time, it may be very difficult to achieve this goal. In many states, colleges and universities also are experiencing significant growth in enrollment. They are implementing numerous strategies to accommodate the influx of new students, such as offering courses year-round and over the Internet. One of the most efficient, cost-effective ways to accommodate growth is to lower time-to-degree. If students move through their academic programs efficiently, they will graduate and make room for new students. When students carry less than a full-time load, however, they extend their time-to-degree, placing additional strain on campus resources. Helping students make wise financial decisions will pay dividends not only for individual students but also for institutions.

In sum, the five choices that appear to affect student success are type of institution attended, attendance status, housing arrangement, student loans, and employment. The message these data send is that the traditional choices—living on campus and studying full-time—remain the factors most associated with academic success. Of course, this traditional approach is expensive, but it pays off in the long run in several ways: increased likelihood of graduation, shorter time-to-degree, and lower opportunity costs. For many low-income students, family obligations put these choices out of reach: one-third of low-income freshmen are independent students with dependents. Nonetheless, two-thirds of low-income freshmen do not have dependents; thus, more students in this income category conceivably could make at least some of the choices that are associated with degree attainment if they had better information about how their decisions can affect their academic progress.

Many middle- and upper-income students could choose to work less and take out student loans to pay their expenses. Given the higher unmet need of low-income students, it is illogical that middle- and upper-income freshmen work as many hours per week as their low-income peers. Some middle- and upper-income students may be working to pay part of the EFC because their parents cannot or will not contribute as much as the formula suggests they can afford. Others may be working to support a lifestyle that costs more than the amount estimated in the college budget. In many cases, both explanations may be true.

Another possible explanation of students' work and borrowing choices, but one for which we have little systematic data, is that students at all income levels are compounding the cost of their lifestyle choices by using a credit card to pay for these purchases. The BPS survey does not contain any information on credit card use, but the 1999–2000 version of NPSAS (U.S. Department of Education, 2000) contains several questions on credit cards. The responses reveal that more than half of dependent freshmen that school year had at least one credit card in their possession. (Independent students are excluded from this analysis because, like other American adults, most of them possess credit cards.) Among those who did, nearly half carry a balance each month, and that balance averages $1,400. These debt levels could push many students to work longer hours.

Although credit cards offer convenience, if students carry a balance, they usually would be better off with a student loan instead. There is no data on the interest rates that these students pay on their credit cards, but it is safe to assume that, in most cases, they exceed the maximum interest rate on student loans of 7.5 percent. Moreover, student loan repayment does not begin until six months after a student leaves school, whereas credit card payments begin immediately. As noted, in 1999–2000 more than 50 percent of dependent freshmen had a credit card, whereas only 27 percent of dependent freshmen took out a student loan. Many students appear to be choosing a more expensive form of credit that may be increasing their need to work.

Conclusion

This chapter has described the demographics and academic backgrounds of entering college students and discussed how these students pay for college. It also has delineated the choices students can make to improve the likelihood that they will complete a college degree. The data suggest that students often make choices that are not in their best academic interest for several reasons: to contain the price of attending college, to support lifestyle choices such as living off campus or carrying a credit card balance, and in some instances to accommodate career and family obligations. Students also may make certain choices because they do not have adequate information about the possible consequences and available alternatives. The question that these data imply for institutions is how to steer students toward making choices that suit their individual needs *and* enhance their likelihood of academic success.

For low-income students especially, colleges and policymakers must continue to work on controlling college price increases and improving grant funding so that these students will face lower levels of unmet need. That said, funding alone cannot solve this problem. More time and attention must be devoted to counseling students on college campuses, in high schools and community-based organizations, and through federal TRIO programs, about the costs, benefits, and consequences of making various financing choices. Counseling students to attend college full-time and work part-time is not helpful if students do not have enough available grant funding to make such a choice. However, additional grant funding will be most effective if students are counseled on the best ways to invest that money in their future academic success. Likewise, additional borrowing can only be helpful when students understand how to use the credit wisely.

An important option that campuses can pursue to assist low-income students (and their middle- and upper-income peers as well) is to forge stronger links between academic and financial advising. How often do students approach professors or other academic advisers asking to be released from a class because their work schedule does not allow them to handle a full courseload? How do faculty members respond? Could an academic adviser refer a student directly to a financial counselor? Could an academic adviser help students determine if dropping a course is in their financial—as well as academic—best interest? Is the importance of making the right choices about work, attendance, housing, and borrowing emphasized in student and parent orientation programs, academic advising sessions, and other such opportunities? Do faculty understand how many hours students spend working and the effects of that work on their academic performance? Do students know how to use credit cards responsibly? What special programs are available to low-income students who so often enter college underprepared academically and with so few financial options?

No one answer will be right for all students, but every student can be helped by having a clearer understanding of the costs, benefits, and potential pitfalls associated with the various options. Such a shift in thinking will help individual students reach their academic goals and may free up vital space and resources at institutions that must accommodate a large influx of new students.

References

King, J. E. *Crucial Choices: How Students' Financial Decisions Affect Their Academic Success.* Washington, D.C.: American Council on Education, 2002.

Pascarella, E. T., and Terenzini, P. T. *How College Affects Students.* San Francisco: Jossey-Bass, 1991.

U.S. Department of Education. *National Postsecondary Student Aid Study: 1995–1996.* Washington, D.C.: U.S. Department of Education, National Center for Education Statistics, 1996.

U.S. Department of Education. *Beginning Postsecondary Student Longitudinal Study: 1995–1998.* Washington, D.C.: U.S. Department of Education, National Center for Education Statistics, 1998.

U.S. Department of Education. *Profile of Undergraduates at U.S. Postsecondary Institutions: 1999–2000.* Washington, D.C.: U.S. Department of Education, National Center for Education Statistics, 2002.

JACQUELINE E. KING is director of the Center for Policy Analysis at the American Council on Education.

*Combining broad access with academic excellence
requires academic and support strategies and practices
that pinpoint student needs and target appropriate
resources effectively. Mercy College, a private
comprehensive institution of ten thousand students in
New York, has undertaken a series of policy and
programmatic changes to support both access and
excellence among nontraditional students.*

Rethinking Policy, Process, and Planning to Redefine Quality and Enhance Student Success

*Joanne Passaro, Lucie Lapovsky, Louise H. Feroe,
James R. Metzger*

Providing underserved student populations with access to higher education poses a host of challenges to the public and private institutions that have adopted this mission. Students from underrepresented and minority populations face significant cultural, economic, social, and academic obstacles in their efforts to pursue a college education and attain their academic and career goals. Providing disadvantaged students with meaningful opportunities for success is resource-intensive, and most institutions engaging in this effort do not boast large endowments or cash reserves. Combining broad access with academic excellence requires a carefully articulated set of academic and support strategies and practices that can pinpoint student needs and target appropriate resources to achieve the desired outcomes: student retention, academic success, and graduation.

We at Mercy College are committed to the proposition that success in combining broad access with academic excellence will change traditional methods of evaluating the quality of academic institutions. Today, prestige accrues to those colleges and universities with high standards at input—that is, students who enroll with high SAT and GPA scores. Although we do not take issue with this definition of quality, we believe that it is far too narrow. Education is a process, and all educators are committed to the belief that it can have a life-changing impact. We believe that the quality of this *process*, as measured by the quality of the outputs—that is, the graduates—is the best index of academic excellence, not the quality of the inputs.

New Directions for Higher Education, no. 121, Spring 2003 © Wiley Periodicals, Inc.

Over the past decade, Mercy College, a private, comprehensive institution located in the New York metropolitan area, has undertaken the challenge of proving the validity of this assertion. Mercy serves a diverse population of approximately seven thousand undergraduate and twenty-eight hundred graduate students whose demographics mirror the college population of the future: approximately 68 percent of Mercy students are ethnic and racial minorities, 70 percent are women, and the average age is twenty-nine. More than 80 percent are first-generation college students, and most juggle competing work and family obligations with the pursuit of a full-time education. Academic disadvantage characterizes a majority of Mercy undergraduates: more than 50 percent require developmental work in English or speak English as a second language, and 85 percent of those tested require developmental work in mathematics. Financial disadvantage is also prevalent: more than 75 percent of undergraduates rely on financial aid to pursue their education.

The challenges confronting our students require that Mercy College be agile and flexible in planning to meet their needs in the broadest terms. The college offers academic programs in twenty-six terms that vary by start and stop dates, length, time (day, night, weekend), location, and instructional media. Mercy has five campuses—the main campus in Dobbs Ferry and four branch campuses in the Bronx, Manhattan, White Plains, and Yorktown Heights—as well as one on-line, "virtual" campus. Mercy also operates extension centers in ethnically and linguistically diverse neighborhoods of Brooklyn, Queens, and Manhattan and Westchester County.

Given the increasing salience of issues of access and excellence to academic institutions across the nation, we have distilled some of the college's key policy decisions into this chapter, in the hopes that they will provide a useful basis for discussion of some of the most important issues now facing higher education. Recently, as a new administration began to review the outcomes of academic and support programs developed over the past decade, we learned one overarching lesson: precision in defining the "access" of our mission was key to ensuring the success of our diverse student population.

Access and Academic Policies

In 1994, the faculty and administration of Mercy College confronted two serious problems: students in major programs had weak academic skills, and their persistence rates were low. A 1993 retention study yielded some interesting data, including that student persistence did not differ significantly according to initial reading ability, home campus, ethnic or racial background, or English as a second language (ESL) placement levels. For the period from 1987 to 1992, the average fall-to-spring retention rate for first-time freshmen was 63.3 percent, while fall-to-fall retention stood at 44.2 percent. The corresponding figures for matriculated transfer students were 71.8

percent and 57.1 percent, respectively. Most of the "early attriters"—first-time freshmen who left within the first three semesters—entered with low English (native, not ESL) and math placement levels and were unable to achieve satisfactory academic performance during their time at Mercy. Our graduation rates were significantly higher for transfer students than for first-time freshmen. These data suggested to both faculty and administration that Mercy's general education core curriculum was not adequately developing students' basic academic competencies.

The curriculum committee set out to develop a set of cross-curricular competencies that would be threaded throughout all the courses in the core. They began by defining expected levels of student competence in four foundational skills: writing, oral communication, critical thinking, and quantitative reasoning. This approach was intended to foster student achievement of the general education goals through the explicit definition of expected student outcomes. The committee established four cross-disciplinary task forces to define minimum graduation competencies in each area. Within eighteen months, a set of demonstrable skills for each competency area had been defined and approved by the faculty senate. Toward the end of that period, in 1996, a fifth competency, in information literacy, was added. Faculty teaching all general education courses would assess students in each relevant competency using a grade roster, and students with unsatisfactory skill levels would be offered remediation.

Philosophically, we were committed to a concept of shared responsibility. Students would be responsible for achieving the stated level of performance in each area, faculty would be responsible for developing teaching strategies that would give students the opportunity to acquire the requisite skills as they progressed through the general education curriculum, and the college would be responsible for providing every reasonable means for the student to acquire the necessary skills and support faculty in the teaching process.

In 1999, the provost conducted a review of the outcomes of all academic and student support programs, including the competency assessment program. Some solid progress had been made, including notable improvements in student writing. But retention rates had not improved. There were a number of other problems, including a fall-off in monitoring the ways competencies were taught in courses. But the most serious problem was structural; though attainment of the five competencies was required of graduating students, skill levels were assessed on separate rosters and were not required to be reflected in final course grades. Thus, it was possible for a student to pass all courses and yet remain deficient in some basic skills. This raised the question of how, or whether, we would hold up a student's graduation for poor performance in the "required" competencies. The general feeling in the community was that course grades should reflect competency development as well as content-area knowledge, and that separate measures were neither useful nor actionable.

Since that review, many all-college discussions have focused on developing clear understandings of the needs of our diverse range of students, and precise definitions of the value that a Mercy education should add to each student's life. In 2000 and 2001, three significant quality-improvement initiatives—funded by federal and private agencies for a total of more than $3 million—were implemented to assist us in developing the programs and services that would best serve our students in their efforts to succeed. Each initiative focuses on increasing student persistence and improving academic quality, though the relationship of those two goals varies somewhat across the three programs. These projects aim to improve our performance significantly over the range of quality indicators we have established for undergraduate programs, which include low faculty-student ratio, road access to academic and support services, persistence, satisfactory development through competency-based skills levels, student engagement in the teaching-learning process, graduation, and actualization of students' postgraduate goals.

Each of these programs contains a strong evaluation component. Progress toward measurable objectives is assessed semiannually, and the resultant data are analyzed and used to adjust programs and services as indicated in our ongoing assessment-improvement loop. These projects are foundational elements of our efforts to promote student achievement by clearly defining expectations and outcomes at every point of each process. The largest-scale project, a retention research and demonstration project funded by the Lumina Foundation, has provided an overarching framework for reassessing the entire range of policies, practices, and services that affect Mercy students from recruitment through graduation and beyond. We will discuss that project last, because it leads the discussion into areas beyond academics; the first two projects highlight our continuing efforts to address the problems of weak student persistence and poor competency levels, and the ways we have refined our understanding of the meanings and responsibilities implied by a mission of access.

Strengthened Admissions Standards and the Title V Developmental Project. In fall 2000, the college implemented strengthened admissions standards in order to ensure that students admitted into the regular baccalaureate program had the skill levels necessary to succeed. These tightened standards were designed to work in tandem with a newly designed developmental semester, the centerpiece of our federal Title V project, which is now mandated for all students who fall below our regular admissions standards. The first year of the project has been successful, and it promises to be even better in the future. Of the 198 at-risk developmental students who enrolled in the fall 2000 semester, 148 passed all four courses and returned to enroll into Mercy's baccalaureate program.

This initiative has redefined the access that is our mission: we continue to provide broad access, but we have simultaneously enhanced the support services that the most academically disadvantaged students receive in order to provide them with a realistic chance of success.

Curriculum and Competency Sequencing. As we discussed earlier, one of the lessons we learned from a review of the outcomes of Mercy's competency assessment plan was that the scope of the plan was too narrow, that the *assessment* process was not effective in addressing the broader issue of systematic competency *development*. Based on this understanding, a general education course-sequencing initiative was developed in spring 2001 to work in tandem with the Title V programs. This project was funded with a two-year congressional grant in April 2001, and implementation began immediately.

The project's goal is improved integration of the competencies into the general education and major curricula. In spring 2001, a newly formed competency oversight committee, which included a number of faculty and staff who attended the Kings College Course-Embedded Assessment Institute in fall 2000, divided into subcommittees that focus on two primary goals: a progressive sequencing of competency development that is integrated with a new progressive general education and major program course sequencing, and the creation of new assessment modules that can be integrated into existing courses.

In essence, this effort entails a significant curricular revision without the disciplinary turf wars usually associated with reallocating credits to various academic units. This effort was possible because the general sense of the community was that an expedited process for accomplishing integrated course and competency development sequencing was necessary to ensure three desired outcomes: that students with weaker skills would not be able to enroll in courses before they demonstrated the skills necessary to pass them; that students in upper-level courses would have more uniform skills; and that competency development and assessment would be integrated into course grades, ensuring that students could not graduate with poor skills in the required competencies.

This initiative, too, has put limits on the notion of access—not in terms of which students we admit but in terms of which courses they can take once they get here.

Retention Research Demonstration Project. In October 2001, the college was awarded more than $500,000 by the Lumina Foundation to pursue an ambitious retention demonstration project. The project focuses on the assessment and redesign of collegewide processes and procedures relating to all aspects of a student's experiences. A steering committee, consisting of students, faculty, and staff from across the college, has divided into activity teams focusing on the following areas: student admissions and recruitment; student advising and planning; mentoring and personal support; financial aid; collaborative-experiential learning; learning portfolios, competency measurements, and standards; curricular and cocurricular programming; learning media and instructional approaches; and information technology.

Phase I of the project, a "thick description" of current policies and practices in each of these areas, is nearly complete. Activity teams are now researching best practices and developing data requests and pilot project proposals designed to lead to significant improvements in processes and practices in all these areas. These pilot projects "went live" in fall 2002. One of the primary deliverables of the project has just come on-line: a comprehensive "datamart" that will provide us with a broad range of baseline data and give us the ability to benchmark progress easily as we move forward in all of the academic and support service projects involved in providing excellence and quality at all levels.

Because of the broad scope of the project, the involvement of staff, faculty, and students from every unit of the college, and the emphasis on documentation and data collection in each activity, the retention demonstration project is providing coherence to conversations about quality and student success throughout the community. This coherence, and the engagement of the entire community in this project, are crucial if nonquantifiable factors that will underlie, we believe, the success of this effort. The retention project centers on strategies that involve the college community in a broad view of the importance of the retention plan, and in the responsibility and opportunity that every individual shares for its realization. Many of the activities in the sections that follow fall under the retention demonstration project umbrella.

Access and Motivation

Most Mercy undergraduates are first-generation college students, and most arrive on campus with a limited understanding of what college entails. These students have little idea of the skills they will need to succeed or the kind of perseverance necessary to overcome the obstacles presented by competing obligations of family, work, and education. In an effort to understand the vastly different degrees to which students with similar backgrounds achieve the desired outcomes of a college education—academic success and graduation—we have begun to focus on ways to identify, and develop, students' motivation to succeed in an academic arena.

Motivation and Admission Policies. Although it is a commonplace that motivation is a key to success, most incoming Mercy students would not seem to have the ingredients of strong academic motivation: many have only a vague understanding of an academic environment, most have uneven family or social support for this undertaking, and most believe that a diploma—and not necessarily increased knowledge and skill levels—will be their ticket to a better life. Though Mercy College is committed to broad access, we have realized that admitting unmotivated students onto an academic turnover treadmill that they will start and stop countless times before permanently dropping out benefits neither those students nor the college. Students are left with a demonstration of failure, and the college has lost scarce resources that could have been directed toward assisting more motivated, though equally underprepared, students.

In one activity of the retention demonstration project, we have begun a comparative analysis of the performance of current students in an effort to define "motivation" and feelings of "agency" better among a nontraditional and academically disadvantaged student population. We are looking to understand the differential success of students with very similar academic and economic backgrounds, and family and work obligations. We have also begun to gather data that could assist us in finding the balance of student motivation, obligation, and incoming skill levels that increase the likelihood of success of disadvantaged students. With the assistance of the Human Capital Resources Corporation we have developed a fairly traditional enrollment management survey of all incoming students that elicits a range of information potentially relevant to persistence and academic success. Among these indicators are the following:

- Social-demographic background, including the educational attainment of parents or guardians, and the student's family and parental status
- High school academic preparation
- Academic ability, based on required Mercy placement tests and other available standardized test scores (the SAT is not required)
- Student objectives, including degree intent at Mercy (for example, certain courses, to transfer out, to earn an associate or bachelor's degree)
- Competing responsibilities, including children or family at home, employment, commute time to and from campus
- Postgraduate or career goals

Initially, the information elicited from these surveys will be matched to student records, and we will track students according to each variable throughout their career. However, once we have devised a way to assess motivation—as separate from obligations, clarity of goals, or incoming skills—we will begin to use a separate motivation variable and test it against student performance. Our goal is to gain a better understanding of how to identify and then develop motivation in underprepared students. We also aim to understand and learn to develop students' sense of themselves as agents and architects of their own experiences. We believe that motivation and agency are key success variables, and that understanding these issues in our student population will help us develop more effective recruitment and enrollment management strategies and assist us in targeting the appropriate support services many students require at or before admission.

Motivation and Financial Aid Packaging. As we have discussed, Mercy students face significant economic challenges, and most undergraduates qualify for federal and state financial aid. As we seek to leverage our efforts most effectively to achieve student success through greater precision in admissions decisions, we are also looking to identify and support motivation through new policies of financial aid packaging.

The effective family contribution (EFC) of Mercy's full-time undergraduates is very low. For 38 percent of the total students, families make no financial contribution to their education; for 15 percent of them, the amount is no higher than $1,500. Only 17 percent receive between $1,501 and $6,000 per year, and only 10 percent fall into the highest category, receiving between $6,001 and $9,000. Thus, of our 4,385 students, 85 percent, or 3,717, filed for aid from 2001 to 2002.

The average income of Mercy students is lower than that of students at most public institutions in New York State. Given our mission of access, Mercy has always pursued a low-cost pricing strategy. Of private colleges in this country, we are among the very lowest in tuition; the full-time undergraduate tuition in fall 2001 was $8,950. In fall 2002, it increased by 5 percent.

Until last year, the college had the following need-based financial aid formula for all full-time undergraduate students at the five campuses (TAP refers to the New York State Tuition Assistance Program):

$$\text{Mercy aid} = \text{Tuition} - (\text{EFC} + \text{Pell} + \text{TAP} + \text{Other grant aid})$$

The college employed a different pricing strategy at its extension centers; students at extension centers were offered a third off of the published tuition price and were not offered institutional aid. The extension centers were marketed as requiring no out-of-pocket cost to students; in addition to the lower cost, the college gave these students their books.

In light of the new strategies designed to recruit and retain more highly motivated students, the college has altered its financial aid and pricing policies. In the past, in an effort to promote access, the college prided itself on attempting to set tuition prices so that state and federal aid covered all tuition costs for a large number of Mercy students. Now, however, we are moving to ensure that we enroll students who are committed to the college as well as to ensure that we provide—at extension centers and at campuses—all of the support services our students need. We have moved slowly to increase our price, and have instituted uniform pricing and aid policies for campus and extension center students. In addition, in an effort to capture student motivation, we are requiring a minimum out-of-pocket contribution to tuition of at least $500 from all students. Thus, the new college need-based financial aid packaging formula is this:

$$\text{Mercy aid} = \text{Tuition} - \$500 - (\text{EFC} \times 1.25 + \text{Pell} + \text{TAP} + \text{Other grant aid})$$

In the past, Mercy College strongly discouraged students from taking out loans. This was due in part to fears that a high default rate would occur. It is interesting to note that although we increased the requirement for students to contribute to their tuition cost, we have not experienced a significant increase in the amount of loans our students take out.

At our five campuses, the aid formula change did not have a negative impact on enrollment. But the extension centers, where we had previously offered a 33 percent tuition discount, experienced a significant enrollment decline. It is somewhat difficult to assess how much of the enrollment decline at these centers was related to our change in financial aid and pricing policy, to our concurrent increase in admissions standards, or to lack of appropriate training and understanding of the new policies by the extension center staff.

As we continue to expand our capacity to understand the impact of these policy changes, we have begun to monitor student retention rate by income level. As one might expect, there is a positive correlation between higher income and higher levels of retention. From fall 2000 to fall 2001, the retention rate of full-time freshmen was 49 percent among students whose EFC was zero, 59 percent among those whose EFC was no more than $1,500, 61 percent among those with an EFC from $1,501 to $9,000, and 65 percent among those whose EFC was over $9,000. The retention rate among those who did not apply for aid was 44 percent; the total retention rate for all students was 53 percent.

As we track retention data we look for strategies to improve student persistence at all income levels, but especially at the lowest levels. This is another area in which a way of assessing motivation would help us to identify and target the support services that students often need even before the first day of classes.

Access to Support Structures

At Mercy, as at most other institutions, students' experiences with planning, advising, and support services, from admission through graduation, are significantly and positively associated with higher levels of academic achievement and persistence. Most Mercy students come from families facing serious economic challenges, and few, if any, have academic or professional role models. Although these students have the potential to complete college and obtain professional and leadership positions, they often lack the experience needed to navigate the academic world; this is especially true upon entry.

Most Mercy students have an immediate need for information that will help them plan for the allocation of precious personal resources from matriculation to graduation. Frequently, these students and their families waver in their belief in the importance of college when faced with competing urgent financial needs and immediate employment opportunities. Thus, Mercy students often require advisement interventions before admission, and they require a suite of support services after enrollment.

In an effort to address our students' substantial needs for support, in fall 2001 we established an integrated "praxis center" on the Dobbs Ferry campus. The goal of the center is to provide our diverse and disadvantaged student body with intensive, integrated support services that will provide continuity for each student in the planning, advisement, and support functions of the college from admission to graduation.

Students coming to the praxis center receive one-on-one access to cross-trained, dedicated professional advisers ("praxis mentors") who assist them in overcoming the initial roadblocks that often result in poor first-year persistence. A dedicated, cross-trained mentor is assigned to an incoming freshman and will remain with that student throughout her or his Mercy career, increasing the likelihood that students will get the personal support and advice they need to attain their higher education and career goals. Career advisement now begins upon entry, and students' goals are continually discussed as they, with their dedicated advisers, create individualized programs of study that will enable them to chart their progress toward their goals as they advance through their undergraduate careers. These coordinated, multiyear individual educational plans (IEPs) serve to structure the individual student's goals and establish a realistic timetable for fulfilling those goals within the unique circumstances of the student's life and through the appropriate learning contexts.

Over the next two years, a federal Title V–funded pilot project will merge some students' IEPs with electronic portfolios that will document student achievement. Students who began in the Title V developmental semester in fall 2000 will be assigned to a portfolio coordinator once they have completed the general education core and are ready to begin their major programs. The portfolio coordinator and praxis mentor will work together with students to develop artifacts of students' academic achievements based on their IEP. The structure of the IEP will be used as the basis of the portfolio, and students will be encouraged to begin to make concrete connections between the IEPs, the contents of their portfolios, and their career goals.

On the Dobbs Ferry campus, our implementation of the praxis concept has not been seamless. But despite initial staffing and space problems, which resulted in a less centralized operation than we envisioned, the project has been successful thus far as measured by student traffic and student surveys. We do not yet have retention or academic success data associated with its first year of operation.

Students' positive reactions to the praxis center have helped solve one persistent problem at the college: students would return to their admissions counselors—often the first Mercy representatives they encountered—for academic advice throughout their college careers. This often led to poorly advised students, and consequently, we assume, to poor performance and retention. Beginning in fall 2002, praxis mentors were assigned to selected students *before* the first day of classes, and we used the results of our new admissions survey to offer immediate academic advice and support to those newly admitted students who needed it.

In April 2002, the Kellogg Foundation awarded the college $500,000 to design and implement a praxis center on our new Manhattan campus at

Herald Square. This center will serve students at the Manhattan hub campus and its five associated extension centers. The Manhattan center will be the most thorough implementation of the praxis concept, because dedicated praxis space has been designed into the renovation and new personnel will be hired and trained according to the praxis model. The Kellogg Manhattan praxis project will offer important and innovative services to some of the most at-risk students at the college—those who enroll at the extension centers.

In addition to the praxis project, the college's learning centers have centralized their academic support functions, providing one-stop access to math and writing labs, tutors, study skills, and other academic support workshops. In the past, these academic support services of the college were both atomized and stigmatized. The learning center and the testing and tutoring office were located in a basement of a building at the far end of the campus. The math and writing labs were in separate offices in the main building of the college, seemingly unconnected to each other or the learning center. The messages conveyed to students about the relative lack of centrality of these services helped reinforce their reluctance to seek academic support. This, in turn, created a significant structural problem for the college, because, as already noted, the five skills-based competencies are a graduation requirement but students were resistant to seek the appropriate help. Though internal data indicated that a student who came to the learning center at least once was nearly four times more likely to graduate, many students did not take advantage of these services.

In spring 2001, the functions of the learning centers began to be centralized. Student usage increased significantly: in spring and fall 2000, the five campus learning centers served 1,521 students; in spring and fall 2001, they served 2,143 students. In spring 2002, a vibrant new learning center opened in a heavily trafficked hall of the main building in Dobbs Ferry. In the first six weeks of the semester, student usage climbed by 35 percent. We expect that the entire college community will continue to respond positively to these concrete exemplars of the centrality of academic support for all students at the college. And given the high correlation between learning center usage and graduation rates, we anticipate that the new approach to student support services that these projects represent will lead to significant improvement in student achievement and persistence, and that the outcomes will become apparent over the next academic year.

Foundations of Access and Success: A New Planning and Business Model

The vision for Mercy College is that it will become a national model of student success beyond predicted expectations while maintaining academic excellence and access as core values. The college has always sought to keep its tuition low in order to provide the broad access to underserved students that is its mission. As we have already discussed, that *access* has been refined to mean *access to success,* and many recent policy decisions and programmatic implementations have sought to ensure the high quality of every aspect of a Mercy education. But given the low tuition that is a foundation of access, and given that the college is highly tuition-driven (approximately 94 percent of revenue comes from tuition), we have had to become increasingly purposeful in all our decisions to ensure quality in all areas.

In spring 2002, the college adopted a new planning and budgeting process. From this point forward, all college initiatives will be measured against their impact on six strategic goals: maintaining access, providing a high-quality education, ensuring student success, achieving financial stability, developing an active learning environment for faculty and staff, and developing a broadly diverse workforce.

We are in the process of elaborating strategies and metrics for each of these goals; the datamart developed in the Lumina retention project will allow us to develop internal and external benchmarks for each. These goals are designed to work in concert: all college initiatives must drive quality goals as well as support the financial goal, though we may make strategic decisions to implement quality initiatives that will negatively affect the financial goal.

In emphasizing their interactivity, we are setting up a tension among these goals. It is the recognition of this tension, and the deliberate balancing of the inherent conflict among the goals that is now required, that we believe will promote a systemic understanding of the impact of actions and initiatives. Our goal is to ensure that purposeful decisions are taken considering their impact on more than one data point. One of the underlying assumptions of this model is that until we have clear understanding of the interactivity among these goals, we cannot drive toward all of them. The process has engendered an active dialogue across the college, a broad-based qualitative discussion driven by numerical analysis.

The new budgeting and planning process quickly brought to light one key consequence of our redefinition of access: high enrollment alone is no longer one of the college's strategic goals. Based on our vision of combining broad access with student success, we intend to meet the enrollment targets necessary for improved financial flexibility through improved recruitment and enrollment management practices, improved quality of academic and support services, and significantly improved retention rates. Our assumption is that quality improvements will drive retention and graduation rates, which will in turn drive our financial goals.

Perhaps the most significant change in the new budget and planning model is conceptual. The process, a service and accountability model, begins with a reconceptualization of revenue production and ownership; this single change has broad implications and has had immediate impact. In the past, the campuses and the admissions office were seen as the revenue-producing units of the college. Because none of these units was responsible for academic programs or quality, this structure produced a host of unintended consequences for academic standards. In the new budget model, which is a service-based model, the academic divisions are seen as the revenue generators, and academic decision-making authority has clearly reverted to the academic division chairs.

All of the non-revenue-producing units of the college—including the admissions office, the campuses, and all functional units—are now conceptualized as service centers, and they will negotiate with the academic divisions (revenue centers) over appropriate levels of service. This model brings the daily practices of the college in line with the realities of an academic institution: producing high-quality graduates is the primary mission of the college, and the academic divisions that produce those graduates should have appropriate input into the quality of academic and support services their students receive.

The faculty response to this initiative has been mixed. On the one hand, faculty do not think that the language of business is applicable to an academic institution, and they do not like being conceptualized as revenue producers. On the other hand, some feel that this process clarifies the fact that the college is indeed a $70-million enterprise and that we need to manage ourselves like one. Some faculty feel that they were left out of the decision loop, and others expressed concern that the new process—which, for budget purposes, combines the five liberal arts and sciences divisions into one business unit—amounted to a de facto restructuring of the college. Faculty generally agree that that this new model gives more power to academic units than they have ever had, and all faculty support the goal of strengthened academic quality, though not all understand the way that the new process will accomplish that goal. They also recognize that faculty governance structures will have to become more active and take on additional responsibility, and not all faculty welcome that change.

Our goal for embarking on this new planning and budget process is to drive quality from the economic foundations of the college up into all academic and service units. This process will entail a substantial change in a college culture in which decisions were as often based on gut instinct as relevant data. We expect that the clarity and purposeful decision making this process entails will increase faculty and staff morale and their sense of interdependence as they begin to take ownership of individual and departmental quality goals and learn to communicate in new and more empowered ways over mission-driven issues of excellence and service. The new planning and budget process is also designed to strengthen the financial health of the college, so that we can continue to offer and improve on the high-quality education we provide to students from economically and academically disadvantaged backgrounds. Our mission is an expensive one, but we believe that it is one of the most important challenges facing contemporary American society.

Conclusion

The quality of institutions of higher learning is usually assessed on the basis of their inputs: the previous academic performance of incoming students. In contrast, the policy changes we have outlined here assert the necessity for an alternative measure of academic quality, one that focuses on the outcomes of the educational process. The questions Mercy College confronts in providing broad access have forced us to examine the value that a Mercy education adds to all incoming students so that we can ensure that they will have uniformly high skills and knowledge levels at exit. In the decades ahead, societal changes will lead to the increasing salience of these issues for most colleges and universities. We are convinced that broad access and academic excellence are congruent goals. The policy changes we have outlined here reflect our most comprehensive efforts to date to ensure that we reach these goals successfully. We look forward to ongoing discussions with colleagues throughout the higher education community as our institutions continue to assess and redefine the meaning of higher education in this century.

JOANNE PASSARO, a cultural anthropologist trained at Duke University, is special assistant to the provost at Mercy College.

LUCIE LAPOVSKY, an economist and former vice president for finance at Goucher College, is president of Mercy College.

LOUISE H. FEROE, a philosopher trained at the New School for Social Research, is provost and vice president for academic affairs at Mercy College.

JAMES R. METZGER, former vice president and chief technology officer at Texaco, is executive vice president for finance and administration at Mercy College.

8

Efforts begun at Ohio State to address the intersections of finance and academics benefit all students, but especially nontraditional students with complex life circumstances. These efforts have centered on keeping students out of the financial aid office and in the classroom, and on designing programs and services that address financial and academic concerns in an integrated way.

Best Practices in Providing Nontraditional Students with Both Academic and Financial Support

Natala K. Hart

Financial aid, conceived in the 1950s, was intended to eliminate barriers for academically eligible students. As stated in the guiding principles of the College Scholarship Service of the College Board: "The purpose of any financial aid program—institutional, governmental, or private—should be to provide monetary assistance to students who can benefit from further education, but who cannot do so without such assistance" (College Scholarship Service, 1953).

When the policy was adopted by the College Board in 1953, the imperative for financial aid was similar to what it is today. Colleges wanted students to enroll, and they used financial aid—then largely scholarships—as an incentive to attract talented students. This practice grew as more and more aid was offered to essentially this same type of student. John Munro, former director of financial aid at Harvard University, and other thoughtful contributors to the discussion proposed that a more equitable process, dubbed *need analysis,* would be fair, allowing students with ability but without means to enroll in higher education. Controversial then as today was the inference that those with ability but without financial need would not receive financial aid.

Current observers of student aid policies suggest that history is repeating itself as institutions use aid as a positive incentive for high-achieving students rather than as a neutralizing factor for those with limited financial means. The relationship between finances and academics has been a stormy one throughout the history of higher education but became a more crucial issue during the last half of the twentieth century.

Opinion is divided over the effects of institutions' financial aid policies on student and family attitudes and behavior. Some believe that when institutions tore down the wall that previously separated financial aid and admissions decisions, they set in motion a series of developments that have resulted in families now viewing financial aid as a bargaining chip to lure high-achieving students. Others contend that the current climate in financial aid is an inevitable result of rising college prices and broader eligibility for government aid programs. Whatever the sequence of events, students and families considering higher education or already enrolled no longer make a distinction between academic and financial decisions. With college costs continuing to rise faster than families' ability to pay, financial aid and enrollment decisions are inextricably linked. The American Council on Education's surveys on public concerns about higher education document that financing worries moved ahead of concerns about admissions standards in the late 1990s. In the years since, this margin likely has only widened.

Today, it is a much more complex undertaking for students to choose an academic program and figure out how to finance that choice than back when financial aid was originally devised. Students are more diverse in their family structures. More than half of the nation's students today are twenty-five or older, married, or have children; these are the federal lines of demarcation between students who are dependent on their parents and those whose personal income alone is considered by the financial aid system. Once thought of and still termed *nontraditional*, these students are in the majority today. Older students have the full set of college expenses borne by traditional-age students, but they also often have family responsibilities. In addition to their own children, some of whom may be college students too, many older students are responsible for their aging parents as well.

Students of all ages work more than their predecessors did. Faculty at Ohio State and many other institutions report that employment often prevents students from devoting adequate time to their academic work. There is no solid evidence on the reasons why students are working more, but all suppositions point to some aspect of financing their education. Whether because financial aid is insufficient or because it does not meet their budget and related lifestyle expectations, many more students work and more often work multiple jobs or full-time while trying to complete full-time studies.

Older students also have less outside financial support than younger students, so they rely heavily on financial aid. Many have forms of debt other than student loans that may limit the type of aid available to them. For example, a student with heavy credit card debt may not pass the credit check required for a private student loan.

Efforts begun at Ohio State to address the intersection of finance and academics have proven beneficial to all students, but they are especially important for nontraditional students with complex life circumstances.

These efforts have centered on keeping students out of the financial aid office and in the classroom, and on designing programs and services that address financial and academic concerns in an integrated way.

Keeping Students Out of the Financial Aid Office and in the Classroom

Before considering mechanisms to address the more complex issues of academics and finances, it is important to deliver effectively the fundamental service that is the core mission of every financial aid office—that is, the first matter to resolve is to make funds available to students in time to support registration and attendance.

Meeting the needs of students for better financial aid service has been a goal of The Ohio State University for the last decade. A merged admissions and financial aid structure was separated by function, adding an enrollment management administrator to whom both offices reported. That change was implemented primarily to improve financial aid services and eliminate related enrollment delays. Support came from the senior levels of the institution, led by the president. The charge was to improve service to students, helping to keep them out of the aid office and in the classroom.

The starting point for a new service plan for all financial aid applicants was the calculation of service demand and response. The financial aid office made a systemic effort to calculate the demand for service in each of its components and determine the desired response. The top five key areas and related service response levels defined are as follows:

- *Key area:* Awards to freshmen should be available by the date competitor institutions provide awards. *Service response:* Awards are in the mailboxes of entering fall students by April 1.
- *Key area:* To support retention, continuing students should know how their upcoming year will be financed. *Service response:* Award information is available to continuing students more than one week before spring finals.
- *Key area:* Most aid recipients should have their financial aid reflected on their statement of account when issued. *Service response:* More aid is credited by the date of bill production and by the tuition deadline than in the prior year.
- *Key area:* Response rates to phone calls placed to the office should be higher. *Service response:* On average, callers should not be required to redial more than twice to reach the financial aid office.
- *Key area:* Students should not wait a long time to see a counselor, and most should be able to complete processes without seeing a financial aid staff person at all. *Service response:* More than 70 percent of in-person visits should be accomplished in ten minutes or less; the remainder should wait no longer than the time of the average counseling visit.

Staff defined the service response goals based on daily and hourly volume counts, as in the case of phone volume, and by observation of the service level at which students and families either did not complain or made positive comments about the service. Comment cards were part of this process, but staff observation was the more useful tool.

Readers knowledgeable about financial aid operations will have noted that the key areas and service measures are outcomes of the financial aid award process. To meet the service targets, it was necessary to streamline the award processes themselves, in particular as follows:

- Reduce the number of financial aid application records verified by comparing students' aid applications to their (or their parents') federal income tax returns only in cases where differences resulted in changes of federal, state, or institutional awards. This is accomplished using a sampling procedure based on prior year changes to determine where changes made a difference, then applying those criteria to the subsequent year's population.
- Reduce the turnaround time from file completion to award, and from new information to revised award.
- Improve staff knowledge and increase automation of the financial aid award process.

The U.S. Department of Education Quality Assurance Program (QAP), which was designed to help campuses identify ways to streamline and improve financial aid processing, provided the method to solve the problem of verifying aid applications through IRS 1040 form review. Ohio State previously reviewed more than twenty-one thousand tax returns each year, with the majority of this work occurring between April 15 and August 31. No analysis had been done to determine when discrepancies between the tax form and financial aid application actually resulted in changed student awards. Software available through QAP allowed us to conduct that analysis. Staff identified those data elements that, although prone to error, rarely resulted in changed awards. For example, financial aid administrators had observed high levels of error in the reporting of the earned income tax credit. Through the QAP analysis, it became apparent that, despite these many errors, there was little change in the aid students were entitled to receive. Such analysis continues to be useful in eliminating a bottleneck in the award system.

At Ohio State, where weekly phone and in-person counseling visits during peak periods number twenty thousand, anecdotal reporting can be very misleading. Few students completed service evaluation cards, and although the responses made were very carefully considered, the ratings tended to be either very high or very low. Now when a student interacts with the aid office, the nature and resolution of the student's inquiry is recorded so that the reasons for the initial problem can be tabulated, and then analyses can be performed to map inquiries back to the student's demographic profile. This method will be effective in identifying policy issues such as inadequate budgets for students with families; if the analysis shows a disproportionately high number of students seeking and receiving budget adjustments, staff will reexamine the budgets for this group of students. Especially in light of the historically low attention paid to independent student budgets and need formulas noted earlier, this analysis could be very helpful to the college's aid office.

"Keeping students out of the financial aid office" may sound harsh, but the idea is actually to allow students to experience a financial aid process that is as simple as possible. Improvements in the process of applying for and receiving aid, although laudable, have not created a process that is understandable to many of the students whom the system was intended to serve first and best. It is not the purpose of this chapter to detail the compelling rationale for an easier, fairer national system of financing higher education. But this goal should not be forgotten as perhaps the best way to ensure academic access.

At the campus level, much can be done to eliminate the need for students to spend time in the aid office. Automation, especially Web technologies, provide ways to assist students more transparently than was the case even a decade ago. However, the experience in financial aid is similar to that of other service industries: the application of technology has failed to reduce staff resource demands. In large part, this is because demand for financial aid has increased substantially during the period when automation has been applied.

At Ohio State, the number of inquiries responded to today is five times that of five years ago, with much of the growth coming through direct student access to information—at first, through interactive voice response phones, and now through Web services. The number of in-person calls has remained the same, but the skills and time required of staff have grown. In a recent survey, more than 58 percent of students calling The Ohio State Office of Student Financial Aid had already checked their personal information on the Web and needed answers to more complex questions. Rather than merely letting students know if their applications are there, staff more frequently deal with complicated aid eligibility issues relating to divorce, estrangement, and loss of employment. This is a common experience in financial aid offices after the application of technology.

These basic service issues must be addressed to achieve a system that helps students stay out of the financial aid office—unless they have a complex circumstance not well addressed by the basic financial aid process—and in the classroom.

Going Beyond the Basics

It is clear that many students have insufficient information about fundamental financial issues (see Chapter Six, by Jacqueline King, in this volume). Although potentially damaging to both the educational aspirations and the progress of a traditional-age student, lack of financial skills can end the college pursuits of older students altogether because of their greater financial sensitivity.

Personal Finance Minicourses. Through a new First Year Experience program and as part of a larger, quarter-long series, the financial aid office now provides this fundamental education to new students. The classes are of typical fifty-minute length. Students are not required to take them, so classes are scheduled at times with fewest conflicts with required classes. Course work emphasizes the value of completing a college degree, focusing on managing personal finances, wise and poor uses for consumer borrowing, saving and investing, and how to take best advantage of financial aid opportunities. The sessions have been well received as documented in students' reflection papers written at the end of each course. Evidence of success also will be measured by tracking the retention rate of students who receive this instruction.

Linked Academic and Financial Aid Advising. To develop a better in-person service model, the university established pilot satellite academic advising offices. Undergraduate student government funds additional counseling staff, and academic units contribute space and equipment. One full day per week, each satellite office is staffed by a financial aid counselor. The intent is to have financial aid information available to students at the beginning of the academic decision process.

At Ohio State, the typical process for dropping classes took place in the academic advising office or faculty office. The serial process of recording and acting on that change required the academic office, the registrar's office, and the financial aid office, and it often took several weeks. This meant that the student, who may have already disengaged with the course content before seeking academic advice, had often stopped attending weeks before the "drop" officially took place. The students usually had sold their books back and were truly removed from the subject material. After the several weeks of processing information in this way, a significant bill for financial aid that must be returned was often the result. But in many cases, the student had already used all the aid for the term to meet ongoing living needs and was unprepared to pay this unexpected bill. Therefore, when ready to return to classes, students in this circumstance were frequently barred by the unpaid bill. Our premise in staffing the satellite offices was that if information were timely, a student would make a more solid academic decision; if that decision was to stay in class, the period of academic disengagement would be far shorter.

As is so often the case with pilot activities, many additional issues and solutions arose from the model. Academic advisers in the units with financial aid staff available have become far more knowledgeable about financial aid. They refer students more frequently to financial aid staff than they did when the process took weeks. The financial aid staff members have become a source of information for all academic advisers as they have had the opportunity to be part of the academic offices on a regular basis.

This staff interaction led to the development of a financial aid conference for academic advisers, which is now in its fourth year. Any topic concerning the intersection of finances and studies is considered. Sessions on financial aid basics and federal satisfactory academic progress rules have become standard. Sessions about how much work is too much work, and how much borrowing is too much borrowing, have been added. Certainly an unintended but welcome consequence of the conference has been better understanding and support of the financial aid staff by academic advisers.

The pilot efforts have led to changes in the timing of the financial aid staff members' schedules in the academic units. On the academic advising day of highest volume, two staff members may be required. In another academic office, it became important to have the financial aid staff day coincide with transfer student orientation. One academic area reserves part of the day when the financial aid staff member is there to discuss cases where finances are of concern. The model continues to evolve in both content and timing. Ultimately, these lessons will be folded into Web-based models to offer round-the-clock information access as students desire. For students who juggle work, family, and college, this service will be especially beneficial.

Unique Needs and Circumstances of Nontraditional Students

Older students more frequently need personal assistance because their circumstances are so complex. Many would argue that the basic system is again the root cause; the financial aid system was designed and implemented for more traditional students who are dependent on their parents' resources, have not been part of the workforce, go to college full-time, and graduate as soon as possible. The additional financial responsibilities of older students and their necessarily more varied academic attendance patterns mean that they often are not well-served by a system predicated on that original model.

Now that older students constitute the majority of those going to college and are likely to be interested in distance education, the time has come to reconvene national leaders to review and revise the financial aid system that serves them. Instead of beginning with the traditional model, using distance education financing as the objective may permit a dialogue to establish a new system that will better meet the needs of nontraditional students whether they attend college through distance education or more traditional classes.

The first topic for such a dialogue might be to establish the student budget on which financial aid awards are based. The current model assumes a standard structure of academic terms and time in the classroom. The distance education model challenges that construct (often referred to as the "twelve-hour rule" because of a federal requirement that students attending full-time receive at least twelve hours per week of classroom instruction).

When the student takes classes over a schedule of variable length, what should the relationship be between time and the budgeted amount for non-educational expenses such as food and rent? Reexamination of this question could benefit the entire financial aid system.

Another example of the benefits of a new look at costs has to do with current financial aid limits. Most aid programs assume that a student does not attend one term of an academic year—usually, the summer—and thus limit annual aid maximums to two semesters or three quarters. For many students, and especially nontraditional students, this model simply fails the test of their lifestyle. Students who attend year-round reasonably assume that they should be able to get aid for every term in which they enroll, but the system currently does not meet that basic need.

Conclusion

Even if the national financial aid system were changed to serve older adult students better, new approaches are required. Ohio State, known as the largest public institution in the country, serves many nontraditional students. Students once perceived financial aid service as a great barrier to attendance. With fundamental service issues being met in a better way, the financial aid staff went back to the financial aid basics of eliminating barriers to pursuing a degree. Staff developed approaches based on several premises:

- Become more evaluative, collecting and analyzing data to ensure policy review based on evaluation rather than anecdote.
- Ensure information about financial impact on academic decisions as close as possible to the time of the academic decision.
- Serve the students (and, if applicable, their families) where they are physically and when it best meets the students' schedules.

The commitment to serve students through timely financial aid service and analysis-based policy and process improvement benefits all students, but those who benefit most are students who have not traditionally had access to higher education. Even at a very large institution like Ohio State, projects aimed at removing financial barriers to academic success prove worthwhile, especially for students with complex family, work, and college pursuits. The results? Improved retention and graduation rates, and fulfillment of the true access mission of financial aid.

Reference

College Scholarship Service. *Manual for Student Aid Administrators: Policies and Procedures.* New York: College Entrance Examination Board, 1953.

NATALA K. HART *is director of the Office of Student Financial Aid at The Ohio State University.*

INDEX

Academic advising: and multiple attendance, 24; of older students, 104–105
Accelerated learning, 59
Access, model programs for, 96–97
Accountability, 53, 66–67, 96–97
Achievement: model programs for, 87; standards for, 39
Adelman, C., 15, 16, 17, 23, 27
Admissions policies, 57, 88, 90–91, 101–103
African American population, growth in, 5, 7
African American students, enrollment of, 4
Alabama, 7, 8, 10
American Council on Education, 100
American Indian population, growth in, 5, 8
American Indian students, enrollment of, 4
Anderson, E., 1, 2, 3
Anderson, V. J., 37, 38, 39
Angelo, T. A., 39
Arcadia University, 14
Arizona, 6, 7, 8, 9, 10, 55
Arizona State University, 15
Arkansas, 6, 7, 8
Articulation, public policy for, 58
Asian American students, enrollment of, 4
Asian population, growth in, 5, 7–8
Assessment, model programs for, 89
Astin, A. W., 38
Attendance status, 71, 73, 81
Attribution, 39
Autonomy, 52

Baby Boom Echo generation, 3
Baccalaureate and Beyond (B&B), 17
Banta, T. W., 39
Beaver College. See Arcadia University
Beginning Postsecondary Students (BPS), 17–20, 26–27, 70
Berheide, C., 24
Black, K. E., 39
Blanco, C., 2, 51
Bok, D., 52

BPS. See Beginning Postsecondary Students (BPS)
Bureau of Labor Statistics, 53

California, 6, 7, 8, 9, 10, 55
California State University, 63
Career advisement, 94
Catterall, J. S., 46
Center for Academic Transformation, 47
Chickering, A. W., 38
Choice, student: and attendance status, 73; consequences of, 80–81; of financial aid, 74–75, 77–82; of institution, 29–30, 72–73; and living arrangements, 73; overview of, 69–70; and persistence, 76–82; and student budget, 74; to work, 75–76
Choy, S., 26
Clinton, W., 61
Cohen, A. M., 13
College Board, 55, 59, 99
College Scholarship Service of the College Board, 99
Colorado, 6, 7
Community colleges, low-income students' choice of, 29–30, 72
Connecticut, 6
Consolidated enrollment, 15
Contract services, 63–64
Corrigan, M., 1, 2, 25
Cost, of education, 54–55, 79–80
Course credits, standardization of, 13
Credit cards, 81–82, 100
Credit-accounting system: development of, 13; and multiple attendance, 23–24; need for change in, 23–24
Cross, K. P., 39
Curriculum, 87, 89

Davis Foundation, 46
de los Santos, A., Jr., 14
Delaware, 7
Delegation, and productivity, 40
Dependent students, 25, 26, 27–31, 32, 70–71
Dewey, J., 44
Differentiated tuition, 55

Distance education: financial aid for, 60; of older students, 105; public policy for, 58–59
District of Columbia, 10
Diversity: and productivity, 35–36; of U.S. population, 5–11
Double-dipping, 14

Economy, 53
Effective family contribution, 92
Enrollment: of African American students, 4; of American Indian students, 4; of Asian students, 4; of full-time students, 4; of Hispanic students, 4; history of, 52–54; increase in, 25; of low-income students, 27–31; of older students, 3, 4; of part-time students, 4; types of, 14–15
Expected family contribution, 75

Faculty: and financing policies, 63; and productivity, 46
Family circumstances, of low-income students, 28–29, 81
FED UP regulatory reform initiative, 65
Feedback, 39
Feroe, L., 2, 85
Financial aid: choice of, 74–75, 77–82; for distance education, 60; effects of changes in, 100; and financing policy, 56; at for-profit institutions, 53; history of, 99–100; merger with admissions office, 101–103; merit-based student aid programs for, 62; model programs for, 91–93, 101–106; and multiple attendance, 23, 57; need-based programs for, 62; for older students, 100, 104–105; overview of, 54; and part-time enrollment, 57; and persistence, 77–82; shared responsibility approach to, 54–55; and technology, 103
Financing policies, 54–56, 57, 60–67
FIPSE. See Fund for the Improvement of Postsecondary Education (FIPSE)
Flashlight program, 39
Florida, 6, 7, 8, 9, 10, 55
For-profit institution: effect on enrollment, 53; financial aid at, 53; low-income students' choice of, 29–30, 72
Four-year institution: low-income students' choice of, 29–30, 72; tuition at, 55–56

Framework for Accelerated Learning, 59
Frazier, C. M., 59
Fund for the Improvement of Postsecondary Education (FIPSE), 64
Funding, school: incentives for, 64–65; and multiple attendance, 23; problems with, 56

Gamson, Z. F., 38
GEAR UP program, 64–65, 67
Georgia, 6, 7, 8, 9, 10
Gerald, D. E., 4, 25
Goals, institutional, 96–97
Gose, B., 14
Government: regulation by, 65; support for higher education by, 61–67
GPA, and multiple attendance, 18–19
Grades, as measurement of learning goals, 37
Grant assistance, 74–75
Grapevine, 54

Hart, N., 2, 99
Hawaii, 8, 9, 10
High School and Beyond (HS&B), 16
Higher Education Act (1998), 64
Hispanic population, growth in, 5–7
Hispanic students, enrollment of, 4
Horn, L. J., 27
Hovey, H. A., 60
HS&B. See High School and Beyond (HS&B)
Human Capital Resources Corporation, 91
Hussar, W. J., 4, 25

Idaho, 7
IDEA questionnaire, 38
Identity, 39
IEP. See Individual education plans (IEPs)
Illinois, 7, 8
Incentive funding, 64–65
Independent enrollment, 15, 32
Independent students, 25–26, 27–31, 70–71
Individual education plans (IEPs), 94
Innovation funding, 51
Institutional structures, and productivity, 44–47

Instructional design, and productivity, 46
Iowa, 7

Johnstone, D. B., 36

Kellogg Foundation, 94
Kentucky, 7, 8
King, J., 2, 57, 66, 69
Kings College Course-Embedded Assessment Institute, 89
Kosky, W. S., 38, 46

Lapovsky, L., 2, 46, 85
Learning Anytime Anyplace Partnership (LAAP), 64
Learning goals: measurement of, 37–38, 39; model programs for, 88; and productivity, 37–38
Learning, lifelong, 61
Levin, H. M., 38, 46
Levine, A., 13
Lifelong learning, 61
Living arrangements, 73, 81
Loans. See Financial aid
Longanecker, D., 2, 51
Louisiana, 8, 9, 10
Lumina Foundation, 88, 89
Lund, J. P., 39

Maine, 6, 10
Maloney, P. A., 36
Maryland, 7, 9, 10
Massachusetts, 7
Massy, W. F., 36
McCormick, A., 1, 13, 18, 20, 21, 59
Measurement: of learning goals, 37–38, 39; model programs for, 89
Measuring Up 2000 (National Center for Public Policy and Higher Education), 56, 61, 66
Mentors, 94
Mercy College, 2, 46, 47, 85, 86–98
Merit-based student aid programs, 62
Metzger, J., 2, 85
Michigan, 9
Miller, Z., 61
Minnesota, 7, 8
Minority populations. See specific minority populations
Mississippi, 8, 10
Montana, 8

Motivation, 90–93
Multiple attendance: and academic advising, 24; analysis of, 22; and credit-accounting system, 23–24; and financial aid, 23, 57; and GPA, 18–19; growth in, 21–22; implications for, 22–24; and persistence, 20–21; and school funding, 23; studies of, 15–20; versus transfer, 19–20; types of, 14–15
Multiracial population, 8–9
Munro, J., 99

National Center for Public Policy and Higher Education, 56, 58, 60, 62, 66
National Center of Education Statistics, 4, 26–27, 31, 70
National Conference of State Legislatures, 54
National Educational Longitudinal Study (NELS), 15–16
National Postsecondary Student Aid Study (NPSAS), 26, 70
Nebraska, 7, 8
Need analysis, 99
Need-based financial aid programs, 62
NELS. See National Educational Longitudinal Study (NELS)
Nevada, 6, 7, 9, 10
New Hampshire, 10
New Jersey, 7, 8, 9
New Mexico, 7, 8, 9, 10, 59
New York, 7, 8, 9
Nontraditional students. See Students, older
Nonwhite majority, emergence of, 9
North Carolina, 6, 7, 8, 10
North Dakota, 6
NPSAS. See National Postsecondary Student Aid Study (NPSAS)

Oblander, F. W., 39
Ohio, 6
Ohio State University, 2, 100–106
Older students. See Students, older

Part-time enrollment: and financial aid, 57; increase in, 53; of low-income students, 30–31; number of students in, 1
Pascarella, E. T., 30, 38, 74
Passaro, J., 2, 85
Pathways to College, 67
Pedagogy, for productivity, 38–39

Pell grant program, 61, 62
Pennsylvania, 6
Persistence: and financial aid, 77–82; of low-income students, 26, 27–33, 76–82; model programs for, 88; and multiple attendance, 20–21; and transfer, 20–21; and work, 77–81
Personal finance skills, 104–105
Pew Grant Program in Course Redesign, 46–47
Pool, K. J., 36, 38, 43
Population, U.S.: diversity of, 5–11; growth in, 5
Premo, M. D., 27
Primary-trait scale, 38
Productivity: assisting students with, 39, 40; components of, 36; and delegation, 40; and diversity, 35–36; effective pedagogy for, 38–39; examples of increase in, 40–44, 44–47; of faculty, 46; and goal measurement, 37–38; and high-cost services, 40; implications for, 47–48; and institutional structures, 44–47; and instructional design, 46; and learning goals, 37; overview of, 35–36; and recruitment, 46; and reflection, 38–39; and retention, 46
Public policy: for accelerated learning, 59; accountability as tool for, 66–67; for admissions, 57; for articulation, 58; for financing, 54–56, 60–67; history of, 52–54; and incentive funding, 64–65; overview of, 51–52; and regulation, 65; for residency, 57–58; to sustain higher education for public good, 60–63; for technology, 58–59; for transfer, 58

Quality Assurance Program (QAP), 102

Rebounding enrollment, definition of, 15
Recruitment, and productivity, 46
Reflection, and productivity, 38–39
Regulation, 65
Remedial-developmental programs, 62
Residency policies, 57–58
Retention: and financing policies, 55; model programs for, 89–90; and productivity, 46
Rhode Island, 6

Schneider, C. G., 23, 24
Schoenberg, R., 23, 24

Self-image, 39
September 11, 2001, attacks, 61
Serial transfer, definition of, 15
Services: model programs for, 93–95; and productivity, 40
South Carolina, 7, 8, 10
South Dakota, 6, 7
Special program enrollment, definition of, 14
Standards, for student achievement, 39
State Spending for Higher Education in the Next Decade (Hovey), 60
Student budget, 74
Students: background of, 39; characteristics of, 1
Students, of color: challenges of, 85; enrollment of, 3, 4–11; growth in, 10–11; model programs for, 86–98
Students, full-time, 4
Students, low-income: academic background of, 27–28; versus affluent students, 26, 27–28; attendance status of, 73; challenges of, 25; characteristics of, 26; definition of, 26, 70–71; enrollment of, 27–31; family circumstances of, 28–29, 81; financial aid choice of, 74–75, 77–82; institutional choice of, 29–30, 72–73; living arrangements of, 73; number of, 71; overview of, 25; part-time enrollment of, 30–31; persistence of, 26, 27–33, 76–82; risk factors of, 31–33; and student budget, 74; and work, 31, 75–76, 77–81
Students, older: academic advising of, 104–105; distance education for, 105; enrollment of, 3, 4; financial aid of, 100, 104–105; financial responsibilities of, 100; past enrollment of, 4; personal finance skills of, 104–105; unique needs of, 105–106
Students, part-time, 4
Students, transfer: overview of, 13–14; types of enrollment by, 14–15
Supplemental enrollment, definition of, 14–15
Support services. See Services
Swirling, 14

Tax cuts, 61
Technology: and financial aid applications, 103; public policy for, 58–59

Tennessee, 7, 8
Terenzini, P. T., 30, 38, 74
Texas, 6, 7, 8, 9
Tierney, W. G., 39
Time management, 39
Time requirements, of students, 39
Title IV federal financial aid program, 53
Transfer: benefits of, 13–14; *versus* multiple attendance, 19–20; and persistence, 20–21; public policy for, 58; types of, 14–15
Trial enrollment, definition of, 14
Tuition: and financing policies, 55–56; for nonresident students, 57
Two-year institution: low-income students' choice of, 29–30; tuition at, 55

Union Institute & University, 44–45
University of Cincinnati, 40–41
University of Nevada at Reno, 15
University of Phoenix, 45, 53
University of Pittsburgh, 14
U.S. Census Bureau, 5, 54

U.S. Department of Education, 4, 17–20, 28, 53, 54, 55, 65, 69, 70, 81, 102
Utah, 7

Vermont, 6, 7, 10
Virginia, 8

Walvoord, B., 1, 35, 36, 37, 38, 39, 43
Washington, 6, 8, 9, 55
Wellman, J., 54–55, 58
West Virginia, 6, 8, 10
Western Commission for Higher Education (WICHE), 64
Western Governors University, 45
Wilger, A. K., 36
Worcester Polytechnic Institute, 46
Work: increase in students who, 100; and low-income students, 31, 75–76, 77–81; percentage of students who, 1; and persistence, 77–81
Work-study programs, 59–60
Wright, I., 14
Wyoming, 6

Zemsky, R., 36

Back Issue/Subscription Order Form

Copy or detach and send to:

Jossey-Bass, A Wiley Company, 989 Market Street, San Francisco CA 94103-1741

Call or fax toll-free: Phone 888-378-2537 6:30AM – 3PM PST; Fax 888-481-2665

Back Issues: Please send me the following issues at $27 each
(Important: please include series initials and issue number, such as HE114.)

_____

_____

_____

$ _____ Total for single issues

$ _____ SHIPPING CHARGES: SURFACE Domestic Canadian

		First Item	$5.00	$6.00
		Each Add'l Item	$3.00	$1.50

For next-day and second-day delivery rates, call the number listed above.

Subscriptions: Please __start __renew my subscription to *New Directions for Higher Education* for the year 2____ at the following rate:

U.S.	__Individual $70	__Institutional $145
Canada	__Individual $70	__Institutional $185
All Others	__Individual $94	__Institutional $219
Online Subscription		__Institutional $145

**For more information about online subscriptions visit
www.interscience.wiley.com**

$ _____ Total single issues and subscriptions (Add appropriate sales tax for your state for single issue orders. No sales tax for U.S. subscriptions. Canadian residents, add GST for subscriptions and single issues.)

__Payment enclosed (U.S. check or money order only)
__VISA __MC __AmEx __Discover Card #_____ Exp. Date _____

Signature _____ Day Phone _____
__ Bill Me (U.S. institutional orders only. Purchase order required.)

Purchase order # _____
Federal Tax ID13559302   **GST 89102 8052**

Name _____

Address _____

_____

Phone _____ E-mail _____

For more information about Jossey-Bass, visit our Web site at www.josseybass.com

PROMOTION CODE ND03

OTHER TITLES AVAILABLE IN THE
NEW DIRECTIONS FOR HIGHER EDUCATION SERIES
Martin Kramer, Editor-in-Chief

HE120   **Leveraging Resources Through Partnerships**
Lawrence G. Dotolo, John B. Noftsinger, Jr.
Provides examples of the benefits of consortial and external partnerships
that have proven to be successful for all the participants. Covers such topics
as leveraging resources, K–12 partnerships, economic development,
community development, workforce development, technology partnerships,
library cooperation, partnerships to serve the military, group purchasing,
inter-institutional faculty collaboration, television partnerships, cooperation
in international programs, and assessing a consortium's effectiveness.
ISBN: 0-7879-6333-X

HE119   **Building Robust Learning Environment in Undergraduate Science,
Technology, Engineering, and Mathematics**
Jeanne Narum
Acknowledging the growing national need for a well-equipped talent pool
from which the scientific, technical, and engineering workforce in the
twenty-first century will be drawn, this volume examines ways that trustees,
presidents, provosts, and deans can commit to national objectives and
translate them into action at the local level. It challenges academic leaders
to take immediate and informed action to guarantee undergraduate access to
programs of the highest quality that prepare them for life and work in the
world beyond the campus.
ISBN: 0-7879-6332-1

HE118   **Using Benchmarking to Inform Practice in Higher Education**
Barbara E. Bender, John H. Schuh
This volume provides different perspectives on the application of
benchmarking in higher education. Authors present conceptual overviews
and organizational examples of how benchmarking can be used in colleges
and universities. The reader will develop an appreciation of benchmarking as
an administrative tool, including a greater awareness of its strengths and
limitations. Administrators or faculty members in higher education will be
able to develop their own strategies for using benchmarking in their practice.
ISBN: 0-7879-6331-3

HE117   **Internationalizing Higher Education**
Beth H. Carmical and Bruce W. Speck
This volume provides insights into how administrators, professors, and
students can promote the internationalizing effort. Thus, chapters are
devoted to promoting the effort by explaining how to help students from
other countries be successful in the U.S. classroom, how to provide
opportunities for native students and professors to work and study overseas,
how to develop exchange programs, and how to help nonnative families
adjust to U.S. culture. For those interested in how to internationalize higher
education, this volume provides a wealth of practical advice.
ISBN: 0-7879-6290-2

HE116 Understanding the Role of Academic and Student Affairs Collaboration in Creating a Successful Learning Evironment
Adrianna Kezar, Deborah J. Hirsh, Cathy Burack
Presents authentic models of collaboration that will help to develop successful student leaders for the next century. Argues that educators must show students by their own behavior that they believe in the power of collaboration, while still acknowledging that partnerships can be messy and frustrating. The topic of collaboration between academic and student affairs is now more important than ever if colleges and universities are to educate students for the new collaborative environment.
ISBN: 0-7879-5784-4

HE115 Technology Leadership: Communication and Information Systems in Higher Education
George R. Maughan
Decisions about investments in information system infrastructure are among the most important—and costly—decisions campus and system administrators make. A wide variety of needs must be accommodated: those of students, faculty, and administrators themselves. This volume will help mainstream administrators think through the decision making process.
ISBN: 0-7879-5783-6

HE114 Developing and Implementing Service-Learning Programs
Mark Canada, Bruce W. Speck
Examines service learning—education that brings together students, teachers, and community partners in ways that foster the student's responsible citizenship and promotes a lifelong involvement in civic and social issues.
ISBN: 0-7879-5782-8

HE113 How Accreditation Influences Assessment
James L. Ratcliff, Edward S. Lubinescu, Maureen A. Gaffney
Examples of working programs include new methods of distance-education program assessment, an institutional accreditation self-study at the University of Vermont, and the Urban Universities Portfolio Project.
ISBN: 0-7879-5436-5

HE112 Understanding the Role of Public Policy Centers and Institutes in Fostering University-Government Partnerships
Lynn H. Leverty, David R. Colburn
Examines innovative approaches to developing the structure of programs in both traditional academic environments and in applied research and training; attracting and rewarding faculty engaged in public service; and determining which policy issues to approach at institutional levels.
ISBN: 0-7879-5556-6

HE111 Understanding the Work and Career Paths of Midlevel Administrators
Linda K. Johnsrud, Vicki J. Rosser
Provides information to help institutions develop recruitment efforts to fill midlevel administration positions and enlighten individuals about career possibilities in midlevel administration.
ISBN: 0-7879-5435-7

HE110   Moving Beyond the Gap Between Research and Practice in Higher Education
Adrianna Kezar, Peter Eckel
Provides suggestions for overcoming the research-practice dichotomy, such
as creating a learning community that involves all the stakeholders, and
using campus reading groups to help practitioners engage with scholarship.
ISBN: 0-7879-5434-9

HE109   Involving Commuter Students in Learning
Barbara Jacoby
Provides ways to create communities that meet the needs of students who
live off-campus—from building a sense of community within individual
courses to the creative use of physical space, information technology, living-
learning communities, and experiential education programs.
ISBN: 0-7879-5340-7

HE108   Promising Practices in Recruitment, Remediation, and Retention
Gerald H. Gaither
Identifies the best practices for recruitment, remediation, and retention,
describing lessons learned from innovative and successful programs across
the nation, and shows how to adapt these efforts to today's diverse
populations and technological possibilities.
ISBN: 0-7879-4860-8

HE107   Roles and Responsibilities of the Chief Financial Officer
Lucie Lapovsky, Mary P. McKeoan-Moak
Offers strategies for balancing the operating and capital budgets,
maximizing net enrollment revenues, containing costs, planning for the
resource needs of technology, identifying and managing risks, and
investing the endowment wisely.
ISBN: 0-7879-4859-4

HE106   Best Practices in Higher Education Consortia: How Institutions Can Work
Together
Lawrence G. Dotolo, Jean T. Strandness
Gives detailed accounts of activities and programs that existing consortia have
already refined, providing practical models that can be replicated or modified
by other institutions, and describes how to start and sustain a consortium.
ISBN: 0-7879-4858-6

HE105   Reconceptualizing the Collegiate Ideal
J. Douglas Toma, Adrianna J. Kezar
Explores how administration, student affairs, and faculty can work together
to redefine the collegiate ideal, incorporating the developmental needs of a
diverse student body and the changes in higher education's delivery and
purpose.
ISBN: 0-7879-4857-8

HE104   The Growing Use of Part-Time Faculty: Understanding the Causes
and Effects
David W. Leslie
Presents analyses of the changes in academic work, in faculty careers, and in
the economic conditions in higher education that are associated with the
shift away from full-time academic jobs. Issues for research, policy, and
practices are also discussed.
ISBN: 0-7879-4249-9

HE103   Enhancing Productivity: Administrative, Instructional, and Technological Strategies
James E. Groccia, Judith E. Miller
Presents a multi-faceted approach for enhancing productivity that emphasizes both cost-effectiveness and the importance of bringing together all segments of the educational economy—institutions, faculty, students, and society—to achieve long-term productivity gains.
ISBN: 0-7879-4248-0

HE102   Minority-Serving Institutions: Distinct Purposes, Common Goals
Jamie P. Merisotis, Colleen T. O'Brien
Serves as a primer on the growing group of minority-serving institutions, with the goal of educating leaders at mainstream institutions, analysts, and those at minority-serving institutions themselves about their distinct purposes and common goals.
ISBN: 0-7879-4246-4

HE101   The Experience of Being in Graduate School: An Exploration
Melissa S. Anderson
Addresses the graduate experience from the standpoint of the students themselves. Presents what students have reported about their experience through interviews, surveys, ongoing discussions, and autobiographies.
ISBN: 0-7879-4247-2

HE99   Rethinking the Dissertation Process: Tackling Personal and Institutional Obstacles
Lester F. Goodchild, Kathy E. Green, Elinor L. Katz, Raymond C. Kluever
Identifies the institutional patterns and support structures that enhance the dissertation process, and describes how the introduction of dissertation-stage financial support and workshops can quicken completion rates.
ISBN: 0-7879-9889-3

HE98   The Professional School Dean: Meeting the Leadership Challenges
Michael J. Austin, Frederick L. Ahearn, Richard A. English
Focuses on the demanding leadership roles assumed by deans of social work, law, engineering, nursing, and divinity, providing case illustrations that illuminate the deanship experience at other professional schools.
ISBN: 0-7879-9849-4

HE97   The University's Role in Economic Development: From Research to Outreach
James P. Pappas
Offers models the academy can use to foster the ability to harness the research and educational resources of higher education institutions as well as the potential of state and land-grant universities to provide direct services for local and regional economic development through outreach missions.
ISBN: 0-7879-9890-7

HE96   Preparing Competent College Graduates: Setting New and Higher Expectations for Student Learning
Elizabeth A. Jones
Using the results of a nationwide study, this volume identifies specific ways institutions can help undergraduates attain the advanced thinking, communication, and problem-solving skills needed in today's society and workplace.
ISBN: 0-7879-9823-0

HE95   **An Administrator's Guide for Responding to Campus Crime: From Prevention to Liability**
Richard Fossey, Michael Clay Smith
Provides advice on crime prevention programs, campus police training, rape prevention, fraud in federal grant programs, and the problems associated with admitting students with criminal backgrounds.
ISBN: 0-7879-9873-7

NEW DIRECTIONS FOR HIGHER EDUCATION
IS NOW AVAILABLE ONLINE AT WILEY INTERSCIENCE

What is Wiley InterScience?

Wiley InterScience is the dynamic online content service from John Wiley & Sons delivering the full text of over 300 leading scientific, technical, medical, and professional journals, plus major reference works, the acclaimed *Current Protocols* laboratory manuals, and even the full text of select Wiley print books online.

What are some special features of Wiley InterScience?

Wiley InterScience Alerts is a service that delivers table of contents via e-mail for any journal available on Wiley InterScience as soon as a new issue is published online.

Early View is Wiley's exclusive service presenting individual articles online as soon as they are ready, even before the release of the compiled print issue. These articles are complete, peer-reviewed, and citable.

CrossRef is the innovative multi-publisher reference linking system enabling readers to move seamlessly from a reference in a journal article to the cited publication, typically located on a different server and published by a different publisher.

How can I access Wiley InterScience?

Visit http://www.interscience.wiley.com

Guest Users can browse Wiley InterScience for unrestricted access to journal Tables of Contents and Article Abstracts, or use the powerful search engine.

Registered Users are provided with a *Personal Home Page* to store and manage customized alerts, searches, and links to favorite journals and articles. Additionally, Registered Users can view free Online Sample Issues and preview selected material from major reference works.

Licensed Customers are entitled to access full-text journal articles in PDF, with select journals also offering full-text HTML.

How do I become an Authorized User?

Authorized Users are individuals authorized by a paying Customer to have access to the journals in Wiley InterScience. For example, a university that subscribes to Wiley journals is considered to be the Customer. Faculty, staff and students authorized by the university to have access to those journals in Wiley InterScience are Authorized Users. Users should contact their Library for information on which Wiley journals they have access to in Wiley InterScience.

ASK YOUR INSTITUTION ABOUT WILEY INTERSCIENCE TODAY!